Work an<

THE RULE OF ST BENEDICT FOR LAY PEOPLE

LISTEN CAREFULLY, MY CHILD,
to the teaching of the master and
bend close the ear of your heart. Readily
accept the advice of your loving father
and faithfully put it into practice, that
by the labour of obedience you may
make your way back to him from whom
you have strayed through the indolence
of disobedience.

YOU are the one to whom my words
are now addressed, who strip yourself of
self-will in order to fight for the true King,
Christ our Lord, and take up the strong
and glorious weapons of obedience.

WORK &
PRAYER

The Rule of St Benedict for Lay People

Commentary by
COLUMBA CARY-ELWES OSB

With a New Translation by
CATHERINE WYBOURNE OSB

BURNS & OATES

First published 1992
BURNS & OATES,
Wellwood, North Farm Road,
Tunbridge Wells, Kent TN2 3DR.

Reprinted 1993

ISBN 0 86012 196 8

Cum permissu superiorum

Calligraphy by Simon Trafford OSB

Composition by Genesis Typesetting,
Rochester, Kent
Printed and bound in Great Britain by
Biddles Ltd, Guildford and King's Lynn

Contents

Acknowledgements

This is an opportunity to express my indebtedness to Sr Catherine and to the Abbess of Stanbrook Abbey for generously giving me permission to use as a basis for this commentary her new and most refreshing translation of St Benedict's Rule.

This is also an opportunity to thank Mr Henry Strick van Linschoten for his thorough critique of this commentary, Dom Simon Trafford for his beautiful calligraphy, as also all those anonymous ones, lay as well as monastic, who have helped in many different ways. Of course all the limitations or errors are my own.

CCE

Why this Commentary?

This running commentary on the Rule of St Benedict is designed to help Christians living in the world to live better Christian lives.

Monks and nuns do not, by becoming monks and nuns, dispense themselves from living good Christian lives. The monastic rules are designed simply to make it easier for them to do so. It is true that the Rule creates a special way of life, separate from "the World" to a greater or lesser degree, but it still remains a Christian way to God. St Benedict found it exceedingly difficult to live as a Christian in the world, so he set up a Christian framework for himself and his followers to live by, based on the principles found in the gospel and on the writings of monks who had gone before him.

Holiness is of course available to all, not only to religious and priests. This was the basic call of St Francis of Sales and was proclaimed in the great documents of Vatican II, especially in chapter VI of Lumen Gentium, *the Dogmatic Constitution on the nature of the church.*

Great numbers of people, men and women, living in the world, have tried to respond to this call to "holiness" and have found St Benedict's words, his approach to living the Christian life, extremely helpful in their own very different lives. This book is designed to help others to share that discovery of St Benedict's discernment and wisdom, his prudence and compassion, his strength which does not crush.

Monks and nuns practise forms of chastity, poverty and obedience not required of lay people, and a specialized form of communal prayer, rarely possible or even desirable in the world. Yet each of these elements is needed in the world: chastity, poverty, obedience, prayer, humility, silence — though in different forms, in new and variable settings. Each of these foundation virtues will be studied in detail as we read through the Rule.

A critic might ask: Why bother with Benedict; isn't the New Testament good enough? St Benedict would be the first to agree. He appeals to his readers to go back to the gospel. Nevertheless, he has brought out certain aspects of the gospel, highlighted them, for our benefit. The same could be said of St Francis of Assisi, St Ignatius Loyola and a number of others, each in their own remarkable way. It is these insights we wish to share and utilize in life.

It would be possible to extract themes from the Rule and write essays on each, distilling the essence of their thought. This has been done many times, though few of the results are of immediate use to men and women living in the world. One admirable example is the work of Esther de Waal, whose books Seeking God: The Way of St Benedict *and* Living with Contradiction *are both extremely valuable in adapting the Rule to life in the world.*

Columba Cary-Elwes

Translator's Preface

This translation is an attempt to present the teaching of St Benedict in clear, readable English. Four things led me to make the attempt: changes in English usage, notably the development of inclusive language; shifts in scholarly opinion – the case for Benedict's dependence on the Rule of the Master no longer looks *quite* as unassailable as it once did; the growth of popular interest in monastic spirituality; and chiefly, the desire to understand and live the Rule better. I hope that the publication of this translation alongside Dom Columba's fine commentary will help others to profit from Benedict's instruction.

Like most translators, I have tried to steer a middle course between stodgy literalism and a vivid, but inaccurate, parallel text. The Latin of the Rule ranges from the workaday prose of the chapters on liturgy to the beautifully balanced cadences of chapter 20, and incorporates a good deal of alliteration. In trying to convey something of this variety, I have been able to draw on the richer vocabulary of English and so have not always translated the same word in the same way. *Scurrilitas*, for example, has many shades of meaning, from light-hearted repartee to lewd and malicious satire: here it appears as "tittle-tattle" (6:8), "clownish behaviour" (43:2), "banter" (49:7), and so on, according to context. Inevitably, exact equivalents for some words have eluded me. The *crapula* that Benedict warns against in chapter 39 has a piggish quality that "excess" only feebly suggests. I have not disdained the homely word or phrase where it seemed appropriate. It may not be dignified to speak of monks being "upset" by an unkind snub (31:7) or avarice "sneaking" into business practice (57:7), but wounded feelings and dishonesty are not usually dignified. Again, the Latin subjunctive can express many levels of obligation: I have translated it variously as "should", "must", "may", "ought", "is to", and "let".

A number of technical terms have been retained, especially in the chapters on liturgy, on the grounds that they are likely to be familiar to those interested in such matters and recognizable even to those who are not, e.g. "lesson", "antiphon". Occasionally, but not often, I have suppressed an *et*, "and", or *enim*, "for", a feature of Latin style which can be clumsy in English. More rarely still, I have supplied a word to complete the sense, e.g. the conjectural "unruliness" of 38:8 indicated by brackets. I hope that in doing so I have not introduced new ideas into the text. (My conscience is not quite clear about my rendering of 5:14, but who could equal McCann's masterly echo of the Latin alliteration?)

It is worth noting that Benedict could be careless: there are two apparent endings to the Rule (chapters 66 and 73), and some abrupt transitions from singular to plural, which I have cheerfully followed (chapters 33 and 43). Yet there is much more evidence of care in composition. Benedict always distinguished, as his translaters have not, between *Deus*, "God", and *Dominus*, "Lord"; between *monachus*, "monk", and *frater*, "brother". (The monk who does not come up to scratch is always called "brother".) I have tried to respect these subtleties without burdening the page with foot-notes.

In some places, ambiguity has been deliberately used. By saying that Sunday Vigils should be "of the proper length", I leave others to debate whether the Latin means that nothing should be added or nothing taken away (11:1). Similarly, is the *improbus* brother of chapter 23 one who cannot, or one who refuses, to understand?

I have applied inclusive language selectively. The Rule was originally meant for men only, but there is no particular justification for the practice of inserting references to "man" or "men" where the Latin is obligingly unspecific and the context does not specially require them, or where an "inclusive" rendering sounds as natural as the "specific", eg. the *senex sapiens*, "wise old man", of chapter 66 is here "somebody old and wise".

The translation has been divided into verses according to Lentini's system. Scripture references and a note of the dates on which particular sections of the Rule are read in monasteries will be found in the margin.

It is pleasant to end by acknowledging one's debt to others. I have consulted the Latin texts of Butler, McCann, Hanslik, Neufville, Fry and, at a comparatively late stage, Steidle. Among elucidators of the text, de Vogüé's name must stand first. Thanks of a different kind must go to my parents, Dom Columba Cary Elwes, Dom Simon Trafford, Mrs Elizabeth Weeks, the publishers and, "above all" as Benedict would say, the Abbess and Community of Stanbrook, each of whom has, in her own way, contributed to these pages.

Catherine Wybourne

The Rule of St Benedict

Prologue

January 1
May 2
September 1

[1]Listen carefully, my child, to the teaching of the master and bend close the ear of your heart. Readily accept the advice of your loving father and faithfully put it into practice, [2]that by the labour of obedience you may make your way back to him from whom you have strayed through the indolence of disobedience. [3]You are the one to whom my words are now addressed, who strip yourself of self-will in order to fight for the true King, Christ our Lord, and take up the strong and glorious weapons of obedience.

[4]First of all, whatever good work you begin, you must ask him most earnestly in prayer to bring it to perfection, [5]so that he who has already graciously counted us among his children may never be saddened by our evil deeds. [6]Indeed, we must always so serve him with the good things he has given us that he may never, like an angry father, disinherit his children, [7]nor, like a fear-inspiring lord, be infuriated by our sins and condemn us to everlasting punishment as good-for-nothing servants who refused to follow him to glory.

January 2
May 3
September 2
Rom. 13:11

[8]Let us be up then, at long last, for scripture rouses us with the words, "Now is the hour for us to rise from sleep". [9]Let us open our eyes to the divine light, prick up our ears and pay

attention to the warning that the voice of

Ps. 94(95):8 God cries out to us every day: [10]"Today, if you would hear his voice, harden not Rev. 2:7 your hearts"; [11]and again, "Whoever has ears to hear, let him hear what the Spirit says to the churches." [12]And what does Ps. 33(34): 11–12 he say? "Come, children, listen to me: I John 12:35 will teach you the fear of the Lord. [13]Run while you have the light of life, lest the darkness of death overtake you."

January 3
May 4
September 3
[14]Then, seeking his worker among the great throng of people to whom he calls out in this way, the Lord says further, Ps. 33(34):13 [15]"Who is there who longs for life and desires to see good days?" [16]If you hear Ps. 33(34):14–15 and reply, "I do", God says to you, [17]"If you desire true and everlasting life, keep your tongue from evil and your lips from deceitful speech. Turn away from evil and do good; seek after peace and pursue it." [18]Then, when you have done so, my cf Isa. 58:9 eyes will be upon you and my ears open to your prayers. Even before you call upon me, I will say to you, "See! Here I am." [19]What could be sweeter to us, beloved brethren, than this voice of the Lord urging us? [20]See how the Lord in his loving mercy shows us the way of life!

January 4
May 5
September 4
[21]So, let us gird up our loins with faith and the performance of good works and walk in his ways, following the guidance 1 Thess. 2:12 of the gospel, that we may be deemed worthy to see him who has called us into his kingdom.

[22]If we wish to live in the tent of his kingdom, we shall never reach it unless

we run there with good deeds. [23]But let
us ask the Lord with the prophet, "Lord,
who shall dwell in your tent or rest on
your holy mountain?" [24]After this question, brethren, let us heed the Lord's
reply, in which he shows us the way to
his tent: [25]"Whoever walks without fault
and acts with justice; [26]who speaks the
truth from his heart; who has not
practised deceit with his tongue; [27]who
has done no wrong to his neighbour nor
believed slander about him"; [28]who has
brought the devil to nought, and hurled
both evil tempter and temptation from
the sight of his heart; who has taken hold
of his thoughts while still half-formed
and dashed them against Christ. [29]Those
who fear the Lord do not become proud
about their own good behaviour but
recognize that they can do no good by
themselves: all comes from him; [30]so they
glorify the Lord's work in them, saying
with the prophet, "Not to us, Lord, not
to us, but to your name give the glory."
[31]In the same way, the Apostle Paul did
not take the credit for his preaching to
himself but said, "By the grace of God I
am what I am", [32]adding, "Let anyone
who boasts, boast of the Lord."

[33]Accordingly, the Lord also says in
the gospel, "Whoever hears my words
and acts on them is like a wise man who
built his house upon rock. [34]Floods came
and winds blew and beat against that
house, but it did not fall because it was
founded upon rock." [35]After giving us
these instructions, the Lord waits for us

Ps. 14(15):1

Ps. 14(15):2–3

Ps. 136(137):9

Ps. 113:9
(Ps. 115:1)

1 Cor. 15:10
2 Cor. 10:17

January 5
May 6
September 5
Matt 7:24–25

every day to put his holy teaching into practice as we ought. [36]That is why the days of our life have been lengthened by way of a truce, so that we may amend our faults. [37]As the apostle says, "Do you not realize that God's patience is urging you to repent?" [38]For our loving Lord says, "I do not will the death of a sinner, but that he should turn from his way and live."

Rom. 2:4

Ezek. 33:11

January 6
May 7
September 6

[39]Now, brethren, as we have asked the Lord who will dwell in his tent, we have heard his instructions for living in it, but only if we do what is required of one who lives there. [40]We must, therefore, prepare our hearts and bodies to serve under holy obedience to his commands; [41]and where our nature is powerless, let us ask the Lord to supply the help of his grace. [42]If we want to escape the pains of hell and attain everlasting life, [43]then, while there is still time, while we are in the body and can still do all these things by the light of this life, [44]we must make haste to do at once what will profit us for all eternity.

January 7
May 8
September 7

[45]We must, therefore, establish a school for the Lord's service. [46]In setting out its regulations, we hope to impose nothing harsh or burdensome; [47]but if, for good reason – the amendment of faults or safeguarding of charity – there seems to be a little strictness, [48]do not take fright immediately and run away from the way of salvation. It must be narrow at the start. [49]But as we advance in monastic life and in faith, our hearts will grow, and we shall run with an

inexpressible sweetness of love along the way of God's commandments; [50]so that, never deviating from his precepts but persevering in his teaching in the monastery until death, we shall share by patience in the sufferings of Christ, that we may deserve to share also in his kingdom. Amen.

End of the Prologue

When St Benedict wrote his Rule, he followed the example of many other writers of monastic rules and made liberal use of his predecessors, including Pachomius of Egypt and Basil of Pontus, Cassian of Marseilles, Augustine and Cyprian from North Africa, but above all a document called the **Rule of the Master**. In fact in the Prologue and the first seven chapters the structure and wording are taken almost word for word from "the Master," though much reduced in length, as the **Rule of the Master** was long-winded. Throughout its subsequent chapters the Rule still shows signs of the Master's writing, though progressively less till the last few chapters. In the Prologue, verses 1–3 and 46, 47 and 49 are entirely St Benedict's own.

For us who want to learn the ways of God, the first word is the most fundamental. It is listen: do not be caught in the entanglement of your thoughts but be open to the word of God, the voice of the true master, God, and Jesus, God's Word. Do what he tells you.

The Prologue begins with obedience; from it all of us have strayed, only to entrap ourselves in self. All valuable obedience is to God, but brought to us through many streams: conscience, scripture, the church, circumstances of life, a rule of life.

The Prologue is a good beginning for any great spiritual undertaking. Life itself is the greatest of them all. And we are always beginning life again each day. Benedict makes a widely applicable suggestion: begin every good work with prayer to God; without it that work is wasted. He takes for granted that, at the start, we shall be sluggish, asleep. He is like someone waking up the family: "Now is the hour for us to rise from sleep" (Rom. 13:11). Who knows? God may speak to me in a unique way in my heart this day. God is sure to, provided I listen.

Whoever turns to God, finds God is already there: "See, here I am." This wonderful truth of the ever-present God is basic to the Rule. Notice that the Rule is a gateway to the gospel: "following the guidance of the gospel" is our aim, so the New Testament must be ready to hand, on our desk, by our bedside, where we pray. But all this is no use unless we "turn away from evil and do good." And how? By grace, the grace of God (1 Cor. 15:10).

*Self-help, yes, but God's help first, the patience of God, always
waiting for us to turn back to God.*

*The same theme appears in vv. 29ff: an interaction of God's
grace and our co-operation. But we must ask for that grace: "Let
anyone who boasts, boast of the Lord" (2 Cor. 10:17).*

*Having set down in general what our aim should be – a return
to God's way – St Benedict concludes that we must set up a
school for the Lord's service (v. 45f), a way of life in harmony
with God's will. Nothing harsh or burdensome, though at first a
little strictness. He promises that once the early steps have been
taken, the way will become smoother because love will grow.
Many have begun with difficulty and not a little fear, but peace,
the peace of love, pierces through, once a "way of life" has been
established, flexible as it may be. Courage, perseverance, loving
trust in God: these will be developed as the Rule unfolds.*

*Read the Prologue, then, as addressed personally to you, a
beginner on the way, with all the eagerness of youth, no matter
how old you may be. Here is a chance to begin again. We are
forever beginning again – novices for heaven.*

*Most of the Prologue, as we have seen, is from the somewhat
verbose introduction to the* **Rule of the Master,** *but Benedict has
sifted the gold skilfully from the dross. Three elements are
original to him:*

(1) *The first part, from "Listen . . ." to "glorious weapons of
obedience" (vv. 1–3);*

(2) *The word of endearment, calling his brethren "carissimi,"
"beloved brethren" (v. 19). He had a warm, tender heart,
sensitive to the weakness and longings of his monks.*

(3) *At the end come those compassionate sentences: "In setting
out its regulations, we hope to impose nothing harsh or
burdensome . . . if . . . there seems to be a little strictness,
do not take fright immediately and run away . . . our hearts
will grow, and we shall run with an inexpressible sweetness
of love along the way of God's commandments" (vv. 46–9).*

Beginning of the Rule

1. On the Kinds of Monks

January 8
May 9
September 8

[1]It is clear that there are four kinds of monks. [2]First, there are cenobites: that is, those who live in a monastery and serve under a rule and an abbot.

[3]Then, the second kind are anchorites or hermits, who have progressed beyond the first fervour of monastic life. They have been tested for a long time in the monastery and [4]have learned from their companionship with many others how to fight against the devil. [5]They sally forth, fighting-fit, from the battle-ranks of the community to the solitary combat of the desert. Undaunted, no longer needing the support of anyone else, they are ready, with God's help, to wrestle single-handed with temptations of body and mind.

January 9
May 10
September 9

cf Prov. 27:21
Sir. 2:5
Wis. 3:6

[6]Thirdly, there are sarabaites, an utterly disgraceful kind of monk. They have not been schooled by experience nor tried by any rule "as gold is tried in the furnace" but are by nature as impressionable as lead. [7]In their behaviour they still keep faith with the world, and their tonsure brands them as liars before God. [8]They live in twos or threes, or even by themselves, without a shepherd, shut up in their own sheepfolds, not the Lord's. [9]Their fads and fancies constitute their

law. Whatever notions they have, whatever they choose to do, they dub holy; anything they do not like they consider unlawful.

[10]Finally, the fourth kind of monks are those called gyrovagues, who spend their whole lives wandering from place to place, staying as guests for three or four days in one monastery after another. [11]Always footloose, never putting down roots, they live in slavery to their own wills, their own base appetites. In every respect, they are worse than sarabaites.

[12]It is better to keep silent than to speak of the lamentable way of life of all these. [13]So, leaving them be, let us go on, with the Lord's help, to make provision for the strong kind, cenobites.

This chapter might appear to be only for monks: that is hermits and cenobites, sarabaites and gyrovagues; yet "parallel" types can be found in the world too.

The Rule claims that the cenobites are the strongest kind of monk because they live together in community, under a rule *and* under an abbot. *Unless the faithful in the world have some guide, director, counsellor, spiritual friend, it is all too easy to lose the way to God. Without some fairly fixed time for daily prayer – no matter how short – for reading of the New Testament or some spiritual book, a time for Mass, for apostolic work, or for teaching our children to love Jesus, we will flounder. For Christians in the world, their "monastery," community, is the family or the household, the local church and any Godly kinship they have with a group here or there, such as the Oblate movement, the St Vincent de Paul Society, the parish prayer group and the like. There are legions if you look for them. We are social beings, supporting one another when the way is rough. We need the help, comfort, advice and sympathy of others. So do they, our friends and neighbours.*

Modern society has been atomized; first went the guilds, then the church, the parish, and now even the family. All these aspects of life – the spiritual and natural communities – have to be restored and renewed, or else society will fall to pieces. The faithful are right inside that incipient chaos, are pulled this way and that by spreading turmoil, and must help in the restoring of justice and love.

The Rule, distributed throughout the world in another age of chaos, provides samples of justice and love. People gathered round these oases of peace will share in restoring the social order.

The Rule mentions those other kinds of monks. First, the hermits: these are praised highly, but their kind of life should be attempted only after the monk has learned to conquer evil, shoulder-to-shoulder with other monks in a community. In the world also there is scope for this solitary life; it comes to all those who reach old age: their contemporaries and friends, their wives or husbands die before them; their infirmities cut them off from others. Here is time waiting for us to start the search for God in earnest. What an opportunity!

But the hermits in the world, as in the desert, need a guide, under God. The devil is quite as able to disguise himself as an angel of light in the twentieth century as he was in the fourth. Those who find themselves alone in young adult life should normally link up with some congenial spiritual group for mutual support and encouragement.

The third kind of monk – the so-called sarabaites – who go about in two's and three's, under no abbot, no rule except their own fads and fancies, simply doing whatever pleases them: do these have their counterpart in the world? Yes, indeed: their counterparts are all those who are setting up the making of money, or power, or sex, or just "me", as their idol, as the object of their worship instead of God, keeping laws of neither God nor man: "*Their fads and fancies constitute their law. Whatever notions they have, whatever they choose to do, they dub holy; anything they do not like they consider unlawful*" (v. 9).

The last type of monk – the gyrovague – is the one never satisfied with his monastery, footloose, a restless spirit. We have to be satisfied with our own wife or husband, our own family and, normally, with the place and situation we have landed ourselves in (and providence has guided us to). St Benedict's word for the opposite to what this type of monk stands for is stability. Of course, Christians in the world are free to change jobs or move house, but – just as Benedict is saying to his monks: don't keep looking over the fence into your neighbour's pasture; find God where you are – in the world too it is harmful to be continually day-dreaming about the happy lot of others. Wiser to get down to being grateful for what we have and are doing, to making the best of it. Doing otherwise brings jealousy, resentment, distaste for what is.

2. The Kind of Person the Abbot Should Be

January 10
May 11
September 10

cf Mark 14:36;
Rom. 8:15; Gal.
4:6

Rom. 8:15

[1]An abbot who is worthy of presiding over a monastery should always bear in mind what he is called and act in accordance with the name of superior. [2]Indeed, he is believed to represent Christ in the monastery since he is called by a title of his, [3]as the apostle says, "You have received the spirit of adoption as sons, by which we cry, 'Abba, Father'". [4]Accordingly, the abbot ought not to teach or decree or command anything that would conflict with the law of the Lord. [5]Instead, his teaching and commands should work into the minds of his

disciples like the leaven of divine justice.

[6]The abbot must always remember that at the dread judgment of God there will be an examination of his own teaching as well as of his disciples' obedience. [7]The abbot should realize, therefore, that the shepherd will have to bear the blame for any lack of profit that the Father of the household may discover in his sheep. [8]It will be otherwise, however, if the shepherd has lavished every care on a restive and disobedient flock and taken pains to heal its unwholesome ways. [9]He will be acquitted at the Lord's judgment, and with the prophet may say to the Lord, "I have not hidden your justice in my heart. I proclaimed your truth and your salvation, but they despised and rejected me." [10]And so, in the end, let death itself bring the final punishment for these sheep disobedient to his care.

[11]Therefore, when anyone bears the name of abbot, he ought to direct his disciples by a two-fold teaching. [12]That is to say, he ought to indicate what is good and holy more by example than by word. To receptive disciples he should expound the Lord's commandments in words, but to those of harder heart and duller understanding he must make clear the divine law by his example. [13]Without doubt, whatever he has taught his disciples not to do, he must not do himself, for fear that in preaching to others he may be himself condemned [14]and God one day rebuke him his sin, "Why do you recount the justice of my deeds and take my covenant on your lips

Ps. 39(40):11

Isa 1:2; Ezek. 20:27

**January 11
May 12
September 11**

1 Cor. 9:27

Ps. 49(50):16–17

Matt. 7:3

– you that have hated discipline and flung my words behind you?" [15]and, "You saw the speck in your brother's eye but did not see the beam in your own."

January 12
May 13
September 12

[16]The abbot must avoid favouritism in the monastery. [17]He ought not to love one more than another, unless he finds him better in good works or obedience. [18]Somebody born free should not be ranked before a slave who becomes a monk, except for some other adequate reason. [19]Yet for a just cause, the abbot may fix anyone's rank as he deems best. Otherwise, everyone should keep to his proper place, [20]because whether slave or free, we are all one in Christ and serve alike under the standard of the same Lord, since "God shows no partiality among persons." [21]For one reason only are we singled out in his sight: being found better in good works and in humility. [22]The same love ought therefore to be shown to all by the abbot, and the same discipline imposed on all as they deserve.

Gal. 3:28; Eph. 6:8

Rom. 2:11

January 13
May 14
September 13

2 Tim. 4:2

[23]In his teaching, the abbot should always keep to the apostle's rule, "Use argument, persuasion and rebuke," [24]which means that he must be adaptable, threatening and encouraging by turns, according to circumstances, showing now the strictness of a master, now the loving tenderness of a father. [25]That is to say, with the undisciplined and restless, he must be uncompromising in argument; the obedient, docile and pa-

tient he must encourage to grow in virtue. As for the careless and defiant, however, we advise him to reprimand and rebuke them. ²⁶He must not turn a blind eye to the faults of those who behave badly but, while he still can, cut

cf 1 Sam. 2; 3; 4

them out from the root as soon as they spring up, mindful of the fate of Eli, priest of Shiloh. ²⁷For those who are more responsible and of better understanding, his first and second warnings should be verbal; ²⁸but those who are wicked, obstinate, stiff-necked and disobedient must be checked at the very first offence with a beating or corporal punishment, in accordance with the text,

Prov. 18:2; 29:19
Prov. 23:14

"A fool is not corrected with words" ²⁹and again, "Strike your child with the rod and you will deliver his soul from death."

January 14
May 15
September 14

³⁰The abbot must always remember what he is, remember too what he is called, and realize that from one to whom more is given, more will be required. ³¹He must also realize what a hard and difficult task he has undertaken in guiding souls and adapting himself to many different temperaments: one must be coaxed, another upbraided, a third encouraged, ³²each according to his character and understanding. The abbot must so adapt and accommodate himself to all that not only may he suffer no loss among the sheep entrusted to him, but he may even rejoice in the increase of a good flock.

January 15
May 16
September 15

³³Above all, he must not overlook or set little value on the salvation of the souls entrusted to him by lavishing greater care on the passing and perishable things of this present world. ³⁴Rather, he must ever bear in mind that he has undertaken the care of souls for whom he will have to give an account. ³⁵Should he be tempted to complain of inadequate resources, let him recall the words, "Seek first the kingdom of God and his righteousness, and all these things will be given you as well", ³⁶and again, "Those who fear him lack for nothing." ³⁷He should remember that anyone who undertakes the care of souls must be prepared to render account for them. ³⁸However many brethren he knows he has in his care, he can be certain that on the day of judgment he will have to account to the Lord for the soul of every one of them, and for his own soul as well. ³⁹And so, as he is always fearful of the coming examination of the shepherd about the flock entrusted to him and anxious about the account that he will have to render for others, he becomes concerned about his own state also; ⁴⁰and through helping others to amend by his warnings, he finds his own faults amended.

Matt. 6:33

Ps. 33(34):10

cf Heb. 13:17

This chapter applies to anyone in authority over others, not least to parents and teachers.

The abbot holds the place of Christ; he is the instrument of Christ, who acts through him. So too in the world, the father and mother, the nurse and teacher, should act with all the simplicity and wisdom, the firmness and gentleness of Christ. Christ was servant to his disciples, but also teacher. When they strayed from truth or from love, he said so or acted in a contrary way. He washed their dirty feet, he spoke like a whip to Peter, but also looked towards him in the palace yard with boundless forgiveness.

Like the abbot of the Rule, we, whoever we may be, finding ourselves in a position of authority, have the responsibility before God to imitate Christ. Easier said than done. St Benedict does not expect instant success, he describes the Christ-like behaviour of the abbot as acting like "leaven" (v. 5), which would gradually spread through the whole being of the community. So too should it be in a family. But he warns the abbot that the failure of the flock will be his responsibility at the judgment seat of God; an awesome prospect. On the other hand, if the abbot has done all he could and the flock is still "restive and disobedient", then the responsibility before God is theirs.

St Benedict emphasises that all monks are not made in the same mould. Some are docile, some not; some intelligent, some not. It follows, he says, that one group will learn by his teaching, others more by example, while some will learn by sternness, by disciplinary action.

This is true in the family as it is in the monastic community: no favouritism should be shown, though good behaviour should be rewarded.

The Rule warns the abbot not to leave any evil tendency to develop until it becomes ingrained and so difficult to extract; it must, like a weed, be plucked out as soon as it appears.

Though no favouritism must be shown, yet each character must be treated differently – and this is peculiarly St Benedict's own way: coaxing one, reproving, encouraging others, accommodating and adapting himself to each one's character and intelligence (v. 24).

In the world one is entangled in worldly worries: money, social functions, the job: they easily smother the life of the spirit, grace, the prayer of the Church – our own – smother just being a Christian. We scold a child for being untidy – quite rightly – but *forget to upbraid ourselves for cursing and swearing; not even practising what we preach, and worrying over worldy matters and not over God's business.*

St Benedict quotes the saying of Jesus (Matt. 6:33) on "seeking first the kingdom of God and his justice". Our Lord did not say "seek only" but seek first, therefore concern for "temporalities" is not out of order. But the first in order is God. All, whether lay people or monks, must seek God above all and in all, not lavish their care on paltry things.

Once again, as he ends this chapter, St Benedict warns the abbot to keep ever in mind God's judgment. "He will have to account to the Lord for the soul of every one of them, and for his own soul as well" (v. 38). So will we.

3. On Summoning the Brethren for Counsel

January 16
May 17
September 16

[1]Whenever any important matters have to be settled in the monastery, the abbot should call together the whole community and himself explain what is to be discussed. [2]After he has heard the brethren's advice, he should reflect upon it, then do what he judges best. [3]Now, the reason for our saying that all should be summoned for counsel is that the Lord often reveals what is better to a younger person. [4]For their part, the brethren ought to express their views with complete humility and respect, and not presume to defend their own opinions obstinately. [5]It lies rather with the abbot to make the decision, so that when he has determined the more beneficial course, all may obey. [6]But just as it is proper for disciples to obey their master,

cf Luke 10:21

so it is fitting that he, for his part, should arrange matters prudently and fairly.

January 17
May 18
September 17

[7]Everyone should follow the Rule as master in all things, therefore, and no one should rashly deviate from it. [8]No one in the monastery should follow the dictates of his own heart; [9]nor should anyone presume to contend defiantly with his abbot, or argue with him at all outside the monastery. [10]Should anyone have the presumption to do so, he must be subjected to the discipline of the Rule. [11]Yet the abbot himself must do everything in the fear of God and in accordance with the Rule, aware that he will most certainly have to give an account of all his decisions to God, the most just of judges.

[12]If the business to be done is of lesser importance to the monastery, the abbot should draw on the counsel of the

Sir. 32:19

seniors only, [13]as it is written, "Do all things with counsel and afterwards you will not regret it."

The title of this famous chapter warns discreetly that we are not here setting up some form of Western democracy, in a world of dictators. The Latin word is not concilium *but* consilium; *not council, but counsels; not for consensus, but for advice; and then not for them, the monks to decide, but the abbot himself alone.*

The Rule does recognize a meeting of minds, if not democracy, as very important: all, young and old, should foregather. All should be given a chance to express their views on important matters, for the welfare of the community is at stake. "The reason for our saying that all should be summoned for counsel is that the

Lord often reveals what is better to a younger person" (v. 3). But this gift of God should not lead to pride or complacency.

This is consultation, not consensus. The abbot is expected to have discernment, to know what is valuable in all that has been said, and then to decide. The fact that the majority may hold an opposite opinion to the one he has come to should not deter him. "Wisdom" is not judged by majorities. If however the wiser sort stand firm in the discussion against his opinion, even though few in number, this should make him move very cautiously.

In this chapter the Rule and the abbot are the foundation. Authority is paramount: no one may contend with his abbot arrogantly and the abbot himself must act "in accordance with the Rule" (v. 11). Endless bickering and this self-assertiveness are not according to St Benedict's Christian way of behaviour.

In big matters all concerned should have a say, in little matters, a small committee is enough, and for decisions, a committee of one is the answer, namely the abbot, "Do all things with counsel and afterwards you will not regret it" (Sir. 32:19). So the chapter ends.

4. The Tools of Good Works

January 18
May 19
September 18

Matt. 22:37–39;
Mark 12: 30–31;
Luke 10:27

[1]First of all, to love the Lord God with all one's heart, all one's soul and all one's strength.

[2]Then, one's neighbour as oneself.

[3]Next, not to kill.

[4]Not to commit adultery.

[5]Not to steal.

Rom 13:9

[6]Not to covet.

Matt. 19:18;
Mark 10:19; Luke
18:20;

[7]Not to bear false witness.

1 Pet. 2:17 ⁸To honour every human being.
Tob. 4:16; Matt. ⁹Not to do to another what one would
7:12; Luke 6:31 not want done to oneself.

Matt. 16:24; ¹⁰To renounce oneself, in order to follow
Luke 9:23 Christ.
1 Cor 9:27 ¹¹To discipline the body.
¹²Not to hug good things to oneself.
¹³To delight in fasting.
¹⁴To relieve the poor.
Matt. 25:36 ¹⁵To clothe the naked.
Matt. 25:36 ¹⁶To visit the sick.
¹⁷To bury the dead.
¹⁸To help those in distress.
¹⁹To comfort the sorrowing.
²⁰To make oneself a stranger to the ways of the world.
²¹To put nothing before the love of Christ.

January 19 ²²Not to give way to anger.
May 20 ²³Not to nurse a grudge.
September 19 ²⁴Not to harbour deceit in one's heart.
²⁵Not to make false peace.
²⁶Not to forsake charity.
²⁷Not to swear, for fear of perjury.
²⁸To speak the truth, heart and tongue.
1 Thess. 5:15; ²⁹Not to return evil for evil.
1 Pet. 3:9 ³⁰Not to wrong anyone, but to bear patiently wrongs done to oneself.
Matt. 5:44; Luke ³¹To love one's enemies.
6:27

1 Pet. 3:9 ³²Not to return curse for curse, but blessing instead.
Matt. 5:10 ³³To endure persecution for the sake of what is right.
Tit. 1:7 ³⁴Not to be proud,
1 Tim. 3:3 ³⁵Nor a drunkard,
³⁶Nor a glutton,

³⁷Nor sleepy,

cf Rom. 12:11   ³⁸Nor slothful;

³⁹Not a grumbler,

⁴⁰Nor a back-biter.

⁴¹To put one's hope in God.

⁴²To attribute to God, not self, whatever good one may see in oneself;

⁴³But always to recognize that evil is one's own doing, and impute it to self.

January 20   ⁴⁴To fear the day of judgment.

May 21   ⁴⁵To have a horror of hell.

September 20   ⁴⁶To desire eternal life with all possible spiritual longing.

⁴⁷To keep the prospect of death before one's eyes every day.

⁴⁸At all times, to keep careful watch over the actions of one's daily life.

⁴⁹To know for certain that God sees one everywhere.

⁵⁰To dash straightaway against Christ the evil thoughts that come into one's heart, and make them known to a spiritual father.

⁵¹To keep one's lips from evil and improper speech.

⁵²Not to be given to talking too much.

⁵³Not to speak frivolously or facetiously.

⁵⁴Not to take pleasure in unrestrained or raucous laughter.

⁵⁵To listen eagerly to holy reading.

⁵⁶To devote oneself often to prayer.

⁵⁷Daily in prayer to confess, with tears and sighs, one's past sins to God.

⁵⁸To amend those sins for the future.

Gal. 5:16   ⁵⁹Not to gratify the desires of the flesh.

⁶⁰To hate self-will.

⁶¹To obey the abbot's commands in everything, even though he himself –

Matt. 23.3 God forbid – should act otherwise: bearing in mind the Lord's teaching, "Do what they say, but not what they do."

[62]Not to want to be called holy before one is, but first be holy in order to warrant the description.

January 21
May 22
September 21

[63]To put God's commandments into practice every day.
[64]To love chastity.
[65]To hate no one.
[66]Not to be jealous.
[67]Not to act from envy.
[68]Not to love quarrelling.
[69]To shun self-exaltation.
[70]To revere the old.
[71]To love the young.
[72]To pray for one's enemies in the love of Christ.

Eph. 4:26 [73]To make peace with one's opponent before sunset.
[74]And never to despair of God's mercy.

[75]These, then, are the tools of the spiritual craft. [76]When we have made use of them unceasingly, day and night, and have handed them back on the day of judgment, we shall receive from the Lord in return the reward that he himself *1 Cor. 2:9* promised, [77]"What eye has not seen nor ear heard, God has prepared for those who love him." [78]Now, the workshop in which we are carefully to perform all these tasks is the enclosure of the monastery and stability in the community.

Of all the chapters of the Rule, this one could be the most profitable for lay people. The list of good works includes: "not to kill", "not to commit adultery", and one may be alarmed to find such instructions addressed to monks; but monks are fallen men, like the rest of humankind, for all their longing for God.

At the root of all holiness are the two commandments of the New Law: Love God with all *your heart, with* all *your mind,* all *your strength, your whole soul; the second is like the first, love your neighbour as yourself (Matt. 22:34–40). The tools of good works are all given to us by God for doing just that: the twofold love. Most of them are straight from scripture; the rest, if not exact quotations, are derived from scripture. The little group verses 10–13 forms part of the stripping off of self-indulgence in order to be free to love without impediments the infinitely loving and lovable God. Verses 14–19 are works of mercy, which have received in our time their stark, urgent meaning. The poor are poor, the naked are naked, the sick are unaided, not cared for in many parts of the world, the dead rot on the ground. Trouble is everywhere. The cries of the sorrowing can be heard from every corner of the earth.* What am I doing about all that?

Jesus said solemnly that we would all be judged by whether we had helped in all these ways or not, because these sufferers are Christ (Matt. 25:31–46). It is among them above all that we find him.

Verse 20 is important, as it reminds us of the opposite tendency in us, namely to go the way of the world, enjoy its riches, its frivolous pleasures, and ignore and even despise the poor. "Blessed are the poor." All those who are ignorant of God, of Christ and of salvation, are also poor indeed, and need help.

Verse 21 To put nothing before the love of Christ, *is the test of our real Christian living.*

The following group, 22–32, in various ways describes how any of us can fail by anger, cultivating a grudge, being deceitful, throwing true love to the winds, lying, doing harm to those who may have harmed us. Patience goes by the board, and as for loving our enemies, or blessing those who persecute us . . . that never enters our heads. So we have still some way to go.

Verses 33–40 are concerned on the whole with the great vices:

pride, drunkenness, gluttony, laziness, grumbling. We may be surprised to find monks warned in this way, but putting on the cowl does not make a monk holy. He is still a son of Adam. All this is equally applicable to lay people. It ends with the commonest sin: speaking ill of others.

After all this depressing list of sins and vices, the Rule suggests, "To put one's hope in God"[41]. This it reinforces by pointing out that it is useless to trust in ourselves, for any good we have comes from God, and it is only the evil that we have a right to boast of. The Rule adds that we must acknowledge this evil, bring it to the light of day. This recognition is so important, because our deep pride wants us to hide it. The great sacrament of Reconciliation or of Peace is made just for this, providing not only occasion to confess our sins but also the opportunity to be healed of these ills by Jesus himself.

44–50: Here is more profound advice, on death, judgment, hell, heaven and temptation. The last must immediately be dashed to pieces on the rock which is Christ, and told to one's spiritual guide. Verse 46 is especially good: "To desire eternal life with all possible spiritual longing."

53–54 St Benedict speaks again of idle chatter and words uttered merely to raise a shriek of laughter.

55: Holy Reading. We have plenty of newspapers, radios, television sets, video tapes. We do not have time for holy reading, Bible-pondering, an occupation encouraged by all the saints. This is followed by a group on prayer, 56–59.

60–61: Hate self-will; not your will, which God gave you and is good, but turning it rather instead from ourselves to God.

62: What is the value of being called holy and not being so? St Benedict simply advises us to live by God's commandments every day, not just when we feel like it or the whim seizes us (63).

64–69: Next come some basic virtues and vices: chastity, no hatred or envy, jealousy, quarrelling or arrogance, and to sum up: "To revere the old"(70) and "To love the young"(71). As well as, "To pray for one's enemies in the love of Christ"(72), and finally, ". . . never to despair of God's mercy"(74).

St Benedict sees these "tools" as gifts from God to be used for our salvation and God's glory. It calls to mind one of the moving plays of Calderón in which the first scene is God giving each one tools for living by; the second shows how each uses these gifts or misuses them; and in the third, the players return their gifts to God and God rewards them or punishes. In the Rule the stage is the monastery and stability in the Community, in Calderón it is all the world, "El Gran Teatro del Mundo", the vast theatre of the world. A lay person in that "vast theatre", that is the world, will certainly find help from the tools of good works here listed.

5. On Obedience

January 22
May 23
September 22

[1]The first step of humility is obedience without delay. [2]This is as it should be for those who hold nothing dearer to them than Christ. [3]Because of the holy service they have professed, or for fear of hell, or on account of the glory of eternal life, [4]as soon as the superior issues an order, they treat it as God's command and do not dally in carrying it out. [5]Of such people

Ps. 17(18):45

the Lord remarks, "As soon as he heard me, he obeyed me", [6]and again, to

Luke 10:16

teachers he says, "Whoever listens to you, listens to me."

[7]People like these straightaway let go their own concerns, surrender their own will [8]and drop whatever they have in hand, leaving it unfinished. With the close tread of obedience they follow up with their actions the voice of him who commands; [9]and almost at the very instant that the master's order is given, the work of the disciple is completed in the promptness of the fear of God, [10]both actions being rapidly accomplished in one by those whom love spurs on to

attain everlasting life. [11]For that reason they choose the strait way, of which the

Matt. 7:14

Lord declares, "Narrow is the way that leads to life." [12]No longer living by their own lights, in subjection to their own desires and appetites, but directing their course according to the judgment and authority of another, they live in monasteries and desire to have an abbot over them. [13]Without doubt, people like these act in accordance with that saying

John 6:38

of the Lord in which he declares, "I came not to do my own will, but the will of him who sent me."

January 23
May 24
September 23

[14]Yet this same obedience will be acceptable to God and welcome to others only if the command is fulfilled without any fear or foot-dragging or faint-heartedness, without any grumbling or raising of objections, [15]since the obedience shown to superiors is given to God.

Luke 10:16

As he himself said, "Whoever listens to you, listens to me." [16]Moreover, disciples ought to give their obedience gladly,

2 Cor. 9:7

because "God loves a cheerful giver." [17]But if a disciple obeys with bad grace and grumbles – not only out loud but even in his heart – then, [18]even if he does comply with the order, his action will not find acceptance with God, who sees that he is grumbling inwardly. [19]He will obtain no grace in return for such work. On the contrary, he will incur punishment for grumbling unless he repents and makes amends.

Obedience comes from ob a prefix that here intensifies the second half of the word whose origin is the Latin word for "to listen"; therefore its original basic meaning was "to listen intently". Obedience here really means to listen intently to the superior of the community, to the abbot, in order to do his will.

St Benedict immediately gives the reason: because they "hold nothing dearer to them than Christ". For monks, to obey the abbot is to obey Christ, because the abbot represents Christ. St Benedict more than once quotes Christ: "Whoever listens to you, listens to me" (Luke 10:16).

For St Benedict this reason is the great one: union of will with the will of Christ, that is love. Of course other reasons are given, but that is the root reason. No doubt also an abbot can go beyond his rights; and what is wrong or evil should not be obeyed. Yet all that happens is under divine providence and God's wise guidance of the world, and this includes commands of superiors, because they are (or should be) sharing in the divine government of the world, particularly those who have been approved as such and appointed by the Church, the local bishop and Rome. Obviously not all the words of an abbot or bishop or even a pope are the very words of Christ himself; still less so are those of a superior in the world. Nevertheless, in the world it is good if one can recognize divine providence in decisions. It is important for lay people to hear the voice of Christ in their priest, their bishop, and the Holy Father. This is also true of obeying one another in love. Christ is in us all and we should rejoice in listening and obeying one another: husbands and wives, children, friends, the small community in which we live.

This sounds splendid on paper, but bishops and parish priests and assistants – even the pope – can be awkward at times; so can the faithful. Much discernment therefore is needed, and patience, prudence, humility and good humour and love.

Verses 8 and 9 are the signs of the readiness of heart to obey, "almost at the very instant that the master's order is given", and as soon as it is given, it "is completed . . . in promptness".

Verse 10: Love must be the motive, and a longing to know or do God's will. The Rule is cautious about our whims and appetites.

Here again: if the command is carried out sluggishly, half-heartedly, grumbling, these are signs of lack of love for God in our obedience. Note what is done sluggishly. We may follow Christ's law on the surface, speedily enough; it is our real inward intention that matters.

All our life is full of obediences, to the climate, our health, deaths, "happenings", calamities, everyday occurrences, friendship, enmities. All these come under the heading of "doing" in these circumstances, or "accepting" with love God's will in them. Likewise, the framework of society in which we live creates a kind of opportunity for obedience: to just government, national or local, to industry, to the extended family, in our home. We expect to obey and also to be obeyed, but it should be as Christians – in love for God as his will is manifested in all these occasions.

January 24
May 25
September 24

6. On Restraint in Speech

Ps 38(39): 2–3

[1]Let us do as the prophet says, "I said, I will be watchful of my ways, for fear I should sin with my tongue; I have set a guard over my mouth; I have kept utterly silent, and have been humbled and have refrained even from good words." [2]Here the prophet makes plain that if we should sometimes refrain from speaking good words for the sake of silence, how much more ought we to abstain from evil speech on account of the punishment that sin incurs! [3]Indeed, because silence is so important, leave to speak should seldom be granted even to exemplary disciples, no matter how good, holy or edifying their conversation, [4]since it is written, "In a flood of words you will not escape sin" [5]and further, "Life and death lie in the power of the tongue." [6]It is for

Prov. 10:19
Prov. 18:21

the master to speak and teach; and for the disciple to keep quiet and listen.

[7]Accordingly, if anything has to be asked from a superior, it should be requested with complete humility and respectful submission. [8]But as for mere tittle-tattle, or frivolous and facetious talk, we ban it at all times and in all places and do not permit a disciple to open his mouth for such conversation.

Silence, a tendency to silence, restraint in speaking, are all contained in that very Latin word taciturnitas. *This is one of the most curious chapters, as the author extols the virtue of silence, obviously to keep from evil words, but also to keep from good words, as he says they could lead to evil ones. He scarcely mentions the real reason why silence is so important, he is so anxious to clamp down on evil talk: vulgarity, gossip and frivolous chatter. Yet he does in the end explain very succinctly. He says it is the place of the master to speak and for the disciple to keep quiet and listen. We are back at the very first words of the Prologue, "Listen carefully". To whom?*

The Master is God. All those who teach are no more and no less than God's agents: instruments, spreading God's truth. We must all be ready to listen to God's truth, his word which comes to us in scripture, and nowhere more powerfully and sweetly than in the very words and actions of Jesus, our Lord himself.

Humour is so esteemed among us that we find St Benedict's strictures difficult. Perhaps we should distinguish laughter for relaxing tensions from laughter which scatters the brain and heart, the laughter which makes seriousness quite difficult, laughter which smashes peace by its very clamour.

It is almost impossible to listen to God in the heart when surrounded by flippant, satirical, superficial, raucous or sophisticated laughter. Laughter can be a sign of divine joy within; equally it can be a sign of all the deadly sins: vanity, gluttony, sexual excess, contempt for others.

When the desire for God is strong, it will be the inner self that is happy and at peace; and laughter gives way to contentment, with the delight at God's surprises.

7. On Humility

January 25
May 26
September 25

Luke 14:11; 18:14

[1]Holy scripture cries out to us, brethren, saying, "Everyone who exalts himself shall be humbled, and whoever humbles himself shall be exalted." [2]In so saying, it shows us that all exaltation is a kind of pride, [3]which the prophet makes plain he has sought to avoid when he declares,

Ps. 130(131):1

"Lord, my heart is not exalted, nor are my eyes lifted up. I have not walked in the ways of the great, nor gone after things too marvellous for me." [4]Why is

Ps. 130(131): 2

that? "Were I not humble-minded, if I exalted my soul, you would treat me like a weaned child on his mother's breast."

January 26
May 27
September 26

[5]It follows, brethren, that if we want to reach the very summit of humility and quickly attain that heavenly exaltation to which we ascend by humility in this present life, [6]we must set up a ladder of our ascending actions like that which

cf Gen. 28:12

appeared to Jacob in a dream, on which angels were shown descending and ascending. [7]By that descent and ascent we are undoubtedly meant to understand that we descend by exaltation and ascend by humility. [8]Now, the ladder set up is our life on earth which, for the humble of heart, is raised up to heaven by the Lord. [9]Our body and soul are the sides, so to say, of this ladder, into which our divine vocation has fitted the various steps of humility and discipline that we have to mount.

January 27
May 28
September 27

Ps. 35(36):2

[10]The first step of humility, then, is for someone to keep the fear of God before his eyes at all times and never forget it. [11]He must constantly keep in mind all that God has commanded and how those who despise him will burn in hell for their sins, constantly ponder also the eternal life prepared for those who fear God. [12]As he guards himself at every moment against sins and vices, whether of thought or speech, hand or foot, or self-will or desire of the flesh, [13]he should recollect that he is always seen by God in heaven, that his deeds everywhere are in God's sight and are being reported at every hour by the angels. [14]The prophet makes this clear to us when he teaches that God is always present in our thoughts. He says, "God searches the heart and loins", [15]furthermore, "The Lord knows the thoughts of humankind"; [16]and similarly, "You discerned my thoughts from afar", [17]and, "The thought of mortal beings shall give you praise." [18]So, in order to be on guard against sinful thoughts, a reliable brother ought always to be saying in his heart, "Then shall I be blameless before him, if I have kept myself from my own wickedness."

Ps. 7:10

Ps. 93(94): 11

Ps. 138(139):3

Ps. 75(76): 11

Ps. 17(18):24

Sir. 18:30

Matt. 6:10

Prov. 16:25

Ps. 13(14):1

Ps. 37(38): 10

[19]We are, indeed, forbidden to do our own will: in the words of scripture, "Turn away from your own will." [20]Moreover, we ask God in prayer that his will be done in us. [21]With good reason are we taught not to do our own will, for we dread what scripture says, "There are ways which seem right to humankind, but which lead in the end to the depths of hell." [22]We also fear what is said of the reckless, "They are corrupt and have become abominable in their pleasures." [23]As regards the desires of the flesh, we should believe that God is always present with us, since the prophet says to the Lord, "My every desire is before you."

Sir. 18:30
Prov. 15:3

Ps. 13(14):2

Ps. 13(14):3

[24]We must be on guard, therefore, against any evil desire, because death stands poised by the gateway of pleasure. [25]That is why scripture admonishes us, "Do not go after your lusts." [26]Accordingly, if "the eyes of the Lord are watching the good and the bad", [27]and "the Lord is ever gazing down from heaven on the children of mankind to see if any are wise and seek God", [28]and if our deeds are daily, night and day, reported to God by the angels assigned to us, [29]then, brethren, we must always be on our guard, as the prophet says in the psalm, for fear that God should some day see us falling into sin and made worthless. [30]He spares us at present, because he is merciful and hopes for our improvement. Let him not

Ps. 49(50):21

January 30
May 31
September 30

John 6:38

say to us later, "These things you did, and I kept silence."

[31]The second step of humility is not to love one's own will nor delight in fulfilling one's own desires, [32]but imitate in deed that saying of the Lord, "I came not to do my own will but the will of him who sent me." [33]Likewise, it is written, "Self-indulgence incurs punishment, but constraint wins a crown."

January 31
June 1
October 1

Phil. 2:8

[34]The third step of humility is, for the love of God, to submit to one's superior in all obedience, imitating the Lord of whom the apostle says, "He became obedient even to death."

February 1
June 2
October 2

Matt. 10:22
Ps. 26(27):14

Rom. 8:38;
Ps. 43(44):22

Rom. 8:37

Ps. 65(66):10–11

[35]The fourth step of humility is that, if in this obedience one meets hardships and difficulties or even injustice, one should with a quiet heart embrace suffering [36]and stand firm, neither growing weary nor giving up. As scripture says, "Whoever perseveres to the end will be saved", [37]and, "Let your heart take courage and wait for the Lord." [38]And showing how the faithful ought to endure any and every difficulty, however contrary, for the Lord's sake, it also says in the person of those who suffer, "For your sake, we are put to death all the day long; we are reckoned as sheep for slaughter." [39]So confident are they in their hope of God's reward, they go on with joy to declare, "But in all these things we are conquerors, because of him who loved us." [40]In another place scripture says, "You have tested us, O God; you have tried us as silver is tried in the fire. You have led us into a snare; you

have bowed our backs with suffering."
[41]Moreover, to show that we ought to be
under a superior, it adds, "You have
placed people over our heads." [42]In
adverse and unjust circumstances, they
patiently fulfil the Lord's commandment:
when struck on one cheek, they offer the
other; when robbed of their tunic, they
give up their cloak also; when forced to
go one mile, they go two; [43]with the
Apostle Paul, they bear with false
brethren, endure persecution and bless
those who curse them.

Ps. 65(66):12

cf Matt. 5:39–41

cf 2 Cor. 11:26;
1 Cor. 4:12

February 2
June 3
October 3

[44]The fifth step of humility is to confess
to the abbot, humbly and without con-
cealment, the evil thoughts that come
into one's heart and the sins committed
in secret. [45]Scripture encourages us to do
this in the words, "Make known your
way to the Lord and hope in him"; [46]and
again, "Confess to the Lord for he is
good, his mercy endures for ever." [47]The
prophet adds, "My sin I have made
known to you, and my faults I have not
concealed. [48]I said, I will be my own
accuser and confess my offences to the
Lord; and you have forgiven the wickedness of my heart."

Ps. 36(37):5

Ps. 105(106):1
Ps. 117(118):1

Ps. 31(32):5

February 3
June 4
October 4

[49]The sixth step of humility is for a
monk to be content with the meanest and
most contemptible of everything, and in
respect of whatever tasks are laid upon
him, to regard himself as a bad and
worthless worker, [50]saying to himself
with the prophet, "I am reduced to
nothing and am all ignorance; I have
become like a dumb beast before you, yet
I am always with you."

Ps. 72(73):22–23

February 4
June 5
October 5

Ps. 21(22):7

Ps. 87(88):16

Ps. 118(119):71,
73

[51]The seventh step of humility is not only to admit openly to being inferior and of less account than anyone else, but also to believe it in one's inmost heart, [52]humbling oneself and saying with the prophet, "I am indeed a worm and not a human being, a byword among men and laughing-stock of the people. [53]I was exalted and have been humbled and brought to confusion"; [54]and further, "It is good for me that you have humbled me, that I may learn your commandments."

February 5
June 6
October 6

[55]The eighth step of humility is for a monk to do only what is recommended by the common rule of the monastery and the example of his superiors.

February 6
June 7
October 7

Prov. 10:19

Ps. 139(140):12

[56]The ninth step of humility is for a monk to control his tongue and keep silent, not speaking unless questioned. [57]Scripture teaches that "In a flood of words you will not escape sin", [58]and that "The talkative will not thrive on the earth."

February 7
June 8
October 8

Sir. 21:20

[59]The tenth step of humility is not to be easily prone to laughter, for it is written, "The fool raises his voice in laughter."

February 8
June 9
October 9

[60]The eleventh step of humility is for a monk, when he does speak, to do so gently and without mockery, humbly and seriously, in a few well-chosen words, and without raising his voice. [61]As it is written, "A wise person is known by the fewness of his words."

February 9
June 10
October 10

⁶²The twelfth step of humility is for a monk not only to be humble of heart but also to show humility at all times in his outward bearing, so that it may be apparent, ⁶³whether he is at the Work of God, in the oratory, the monastery or the garden, on the road, in the field, or anywhere else. Whether he sits, walks or stands, his head should be bowed and his gaze fixed on the ground, ⁶⁴while he ponders at every moment his own sinfulness and guilt and considers that he is already at the fearful point of judgment. ⁶⁵Let him constantly say in his heart what the publican in the gospel said with downcast eyes, "Lord, I am a sinner, not worthy to raise my eyes to heaven"; ⁶⁶and with the prophet, "I am bowed down and humbled on every side."

Luke 18:13

Ps. 37(38):7

⁶⁷Now, when all these steps of humility have been climbed, a monk will quickly come to that perfect love of God "which casts out fear", ⁶⁸and by its means will begin to observe without struggle, as though naturally and from habit, all those things which earlier he did not observe without dread: ⁶⁹no longer for fear of hell but for love of Christ, and from good habit and delight in virtue. ⁷⁰This the Lord will deign to make manifest in his worker, now cleansed from vice and sin by the Holy Spirit.

1 John 4:18

In our time, when success is everything, any failure is the ultimate defeat; the virtue of humility comes as a beggar at the gate and is turned away as being completely out of place.

The religion of Jesus is the religion of failure. It sees human history as a history of human failure; its hero accepted precisely that, human failure, to remind us that God is the only success.

Is that a fair picture of human history? Have we not pulled ourselves up by our shoestrings from grain-gatherers and hunters to tinned food and chickens by the million; from taming of horses and cattle to makers of tools; from builders of mud huts to constructors of high buildings and temples; from walking on our own two feet to flying; from bows and arrows to atomic bombs; from herbal medicines to poisonous gas, but also amazing medical care; from persuasion to torturing the mind, but also to counselling; from peace to universal terror; from belief in God to not even belief in self? This is harsh.

So perhaps modern men and women – not the hangovers from the too optimistic nineteenth century – are ready after all to listen to St Benedict on the human condition.

But beneath the squalor of all the above is the basic goodness-in-sin of human nature, ready to respond to love and beauty and truth. Waiting beneath this crazy superstructure of our world, plenty of simple, honest – but frightened – people remain. They are not taken in by the arrogant talk of those publicists and politicians, who, though perhaps unknown to themselves, are even more afraid than the rest of us.

St Benedict's world was a step or two ahead of ours on the way to breakdown. We still have a chance to save ourselves, or to be saved. For the sixth century, St Benedict's, that moment had passed: Rome, the eternal city, was in ruins, the finances of the western empire were in tatters, the morals of the people had crumbled. A new start was needed, one which was not arrogant but humble. The first agent of this new life, though few could have known it, was the Rule, which set down one or two basic principles: the first of these being humility. We would do well and wisely to "listen".

This chapter is divided into twelve steps. It would be a mistake to call them stages, as then we would be forcing the chapter into a shape it does not have, as though in the life of the spirit we pass through a series of watertight compartments, when in fact humility simply has different aspects, and at one time one will be more important for us than another. St Benedict, without saying so in so many words, puts the inward attitudes first, leaving the "humility in . . . outward bearing" to the end.

The more this chapter is pondered, the more it appears as a commentary on prayer. This is true of the fundamental virtues: love, obedience, poverty of spirit.

Steps, grades, rungs, degrees: they all have the implication of a sequence. Verses 6–9 use the image of a ladder, which confirms this feeling of a regular movement, rung by rung, up or down. Yet we should never take a comparison as absolute in all details. Spiritual things can only very inadequately be understood by means of material images.

An earlier writer on monasticism, John Cassian, called the degrees, steps or rungs simply "indications" or "signs" of humility. This is more accurate if less pictorial. They could occur in any order in real life. But St Benedict gives a kind of psychological order, which is tidy if rare in individual cases. The Rule begins from within where true humility lies; the outward expressions, which come at the end, can be bogus, make-belief.

These grades, steps, indications of humility can and should co-exist.

The first step *of humility is the coming to a deep awareness of the presence of God, the permanent Presence. Whether we are conscious of the fact or not, God is always there. God is all-knowing, infinitely loving and wise; but also, as the Rule here emphasizes, just. This leads to a self-examination; the all-holy, the all-sinful. What else have we which is totally ours?*

Every commentary on Chapter 7 must begin with an explanation of the contradiction between the first sentence of Chapter 5, which reads: "The first step of humility is obedience without delay"; and verse 10 of Chapter 7, "The first step of humility, then, is for someone to keep the fear of God before his eyes . . .". Both passages occur in the Rule of the Master, from which St Benedict has borrowed, and no final agreement among the commentators over this puzzle has been arrived at. Perhaps by Chapter 7 it had become clear that at a deeper level than obedience, a step below, was the realization of our littleness before the immensity and majesty of God, who sees all. From this doing God's will, that is, obedience would follow.

The second step *is intimately and logically linked with the first. Indeed the second part of the text concerning the first step is really a preparation for the second, a kind of reason for moving to the second. Since God sees us at all times, we look at ourselves and begin to recognize our selfishness, the waywardness of our will and desires. These need control. This in fact is the second step: not to love our own will. The second is also the determination to improve: again not to love our own will.*

The third *(logical)* step *is to see in obedience a way to be free of self-will, of wilfulness. The Rule stresses that whatever obedience we give, it must be for love of God. Whoever we obey we really intend to obey God.*

For lay people, obedience comes in crowded ways, first of all in obedience to our conscience. There is an instinct, a power within that cries out: this way is right, that is WRONG. Conscience develops and grows with Jesus' help. Obedience also comes through the Church which shares Jesus' life and preserves his truth, and is a safe interpreter of his teaching.

But obedience also comes in everyday living, an obedience to the divine Wisdom, the way things fall out, happenings, things we had no hand in arranging, and which cannot be avoided even if we wished: someone dying, our own sickness, blindness, losing a fortune, or even winning one. Everything in fact is under God's loving care, except sin which is entirely our own doing. Other people's sins, their avarice, jealousy, anger, laziness, while they unavoidably affect us, can, strangely enough, be for our own good, our patience, forgiveness, love. Within the family, mutual obedient love is at the heart of that family's peace. In civil society willing obedience to just laws also produces peace.

The fourth step *of humility is when obedience is hard. It may even go against our personal interests; or worse, it can even be unjust to us. To be ill makes life difficult, to have an uncongenial companion is unfavourable, to be falsely imprisoned adds injustice to the situation. What does the Rule suggest? The translator uses the word "heart", not the mind or the reasoning, nor even the will, but that biblical term "heart", which for the writers in the Bible means the deepest conscious conviction of the whole person. It is no violent emotion, but a realization that all things are to be embraced (welcomed, hugged, grasped) "with a quiet heart" (v. 35). The words almost by their very sound produce peace, yet how difficult this can be in real life. For St Benedict, in this context, obedience is the final act of the will, saying a firm "Yes" to the situation: "Yes, I accept", but underlying this act of obedience is the deep attitude of the heart, at peace with suffering, accepting it. Tacite originally meant silently, so one can also translate, "Silently our heart embraces the suffering", therefore "At peace our heart embraces the pain of it".*

This condition presupposes that there is nothing that can be done to get rid of the hurt. In a later chapter St Benedict gives sensible and sensitive advice on ways, if possible, of rectifying this situation, and accepting, once again, if efforts prove fruitless, the inevitable (chapter 68).

This step strikes one as the true summit of the virtue of humility in the eyes of St Benedict, as he goes on "and stand firm, neither growing weary nor giving up", and he pours scripture texts over us: St Matthew, twice; the Psalms, three times; St Paul, four times. In both the Matthew references it is Jesus himself speaking. St Paul (Rom. 8:37) reminds us that we accept all with love since Jesus himself has "loved us". All this is a typical example of the way the Rule is grounded on the very words of Scripture. In one paragraph there are nine clear quotations from God's word.

The perfection of this step in humility comes in verses 42 and 43 which remind us of Jesus' precept patiently to endure "adverse and unjust circumstances" (Matt. 5:39–41), while the Apostle Paul adds: they must "bless those who curse them" (1 Cor. 4:12).

To obey, to accept, to say "Yes", was the hallmark of Jesus' life, in all circumstances. This is the message of this step: in sorrow, in illness, in loss, in darkness, in dereliction, rejection, mis-judgment, in loss of money, reputation, friends, in failure, in sin, in death, I come to do and accept your will, O Lord.

We are reminded of Brother Francis and Brother Leo in conversation on what "perfect Joy" is, and St Francis' answer: "When you are arriving in the snow late at night after a long tedious journey, and one of your own brothers answers the door, by peering out through a narrow opening of it and then, seeing what looks like two tramps, slams the door in their face: that is perfect joy." This extreme is not demanded by St Benedict who soberly says "bless them" or, in other words, may God care for them.

We all find on occasions that other people are insensitive to our predicament. We feel deserted, betrayed. We should remember the possibility that we have been perhaps as insensitive to their distress. If we were insensitive it would be not memorable for us. The real sin and real hurt is when we are aware but either do nothing, or slam the door in their face.

The fifth step is the willingness to accept advice, the humility to do so, especially to seek healing in the sacrament of Reconciliation. We cannot heal ourselves. Grace is a gift, particularly the gift of spiritual peace, with God, with self, with others. It is for God to forgive. We are free to ask or to hold back.

The sixth step: Here we enter the area of external expressions of humility, which can be make-belief. But St Benedict is not content with words, "I am the worst of sinners, I am a useless servant". He is concerned with actions that express the inward attitude, being content (this is inward) to be given the most menial job, or no job, because one is a beggar, a worthless worker accepting any task given, and then, only then, saying, preferably in the heart: "I am reduced to nothing and am all ignorance; I have become like a dumb beast before you" (Ps. 72:22) but adding that God is still close, God is saying "yet I am always with you" (Ps 72:23).

The Rule, in the seventh step, reaches beyond the natural. We all have an in-built desire to reach fulfilment, a basic urge to succeed; and we instinctively judge whether we are succeeding by comparing ourselves to those around us. Put two small children together who are trying to stand; they will be urged on by each other's efforts – nothing wrong in that.

Likewise we compete in virtue, not in vice. We wish to excel.

In our competitive Western world, we are moved not only to succeed but also to excel, from childhood to the grave. Is this urge to excel a virtue or a vice?

"The Master" has a fantastic section in his Rule in which he urges each one of the monks to compete in the practice of virtue in order that the outgoing abbot will choose the one who "wins" to be his successor. St Benedict cuts this out without comment.

The young must first be encouraged in virtue, in effort, because that fear of inadequacy is very deep also in them. "You are O.K., am I?" But with maturity we become aware of our basic spiritual weakness, and come to know that all the good in us is from God. As St Thomas Aquinas put it, the only thing about us that we can claim as our own is our sin. So what have we to present as ours in this pseudo-competition in excellence? The more we claim in virtue, the more we see how we have squandered this gold, which was, in any case, only on loan to us. So in theory, here, we can put ourselves on the bottom rung below everyone else. But we do not have all the facts. It is not our job to judge others; all we can say is this: "I was exalted and have been humbled and brought to confusion" (Ps. 21:7). How do we know that we would not have betrayed Jesus as Judas did? We have done so in different circumstances. We are always doing so, perhaps only in small ways, and Judas began in small ways.

The eighth step of humility is very down to earth and psychologically revealing. Some of us resent, within, not being outstanding, perhaps resent being passed over; in fact – perhaps not aware of it – think we are a cut above the average. So we instinctively, perhaps again unaware, "break ranks" and do little things that are slightly out of line, start wearing a beard, or sandals, or a peculiar hat, or we behave in church in odd ways; or our table manners are at the least quaint or eccentric. In children, this is called showing off. With us, maybe, it is just a last flicker of self-will.

In the world children must assert themselves, free themselves from over-protective parents. They have to have, sooner or later, a mind of their own – they think sooner, the parents think later. What can be lacking? May patience or humility (in St Benedict's sense here), save us from extravagant demonstrations of independence, like uncouth dress or manners on the one hand, or extremely rigorous reactions on the other. Modern society is full of examples of failure to reach this rung of rationality, truthfulness, humility.

The ninth step *is on silence, and as it stands is very suitable for hermits and monks or cenobites. In Victorian and Edwardian days – the turn of the nineteenth century – silence was thought very suitable for children: they should be "seen but not heard", or speak when spoken to. But all this was for the comfort of their elders. Children must learn to speak fluently and aloud; learn to sharpen their wits by converse, ask the great and simple questions, "Why a cow?" But like the monks, whose silence is for listening, so the children and the grown-ups must learn to LISTEN, to human words of the wise, but also to the divine Word, who is Wisdom. Silence of this kind is golden, worth infinitely more than earth-dug gold. Only silence and listening can bring to light the hidden meaning of life.*

The tenth step *is given to laughter all by itself. There are some who turn everything into a source of irrational laughter, so that they are never serious. Certain people laugh at the most serious subjects, the more serious, the more prompt the laughter. This is simply a nervous uncontrolled emotional reaction. It is what the Rule is describing.*

Laughter can also act like a drug or alcohol. It grows with its exercise and becomes compulsive, reaching paroxysms of irrational shrieks.

The English habit of self-deprecative humour and laughter, exemplified in St Thomas More, could be added as a thirteenth step in humility, for it springs from a due appreciation of how absurd it is to take our own peacocking around seriously. We are comic creatures, unless we weep over ourselves. But God loves a cheerful giver, and a sad one is no saint at all.

The eleventh step *of humility is to speak gently, humbly, gravely, reasonably, briefly, not mocking but softly. All these modest characteristics show the spirit within. It is not those who burst into conversation who are most readily listened to, nor those who speak the loudest, but those who wait patiently for a pause and then speak with gentle deliberation. They get a hearing; or if they do not, those discussing are not able or ready to listen. Even with children it is the quiet voice, unruffled and firm, that carries real authority.*

The Rule has hard things to say on laughter. If St Benedict means one should never laugh, then one might dare, gently, gravely, reasonably, softly and with a smile, to disagree. But the kind of laughter he seems to object to so strongly is loud, proud, arrogant or raucous, thoughtless laughter.

Put the various places together where the Rule mentions laughter, Chapters 4, 6, 7 and 49, and we find that the condemnation is against noisy, immoderate laughter, associated with scurrilous, unmonastic subjects.

In economics Gresham enunciated a Law that bad coins squeeze out of circulation good coins (c. 1580), so scurrilous jokes squeeze out clean ones – as the sneer does honest laughter.

A home without laughter would be like a bottle without wine or a pool without water. Laughter is the expression of joy and peace, of delight and surprise, the spontaneous language of innocence and childhood.

Like everything else it can be overdone.

The twelfth step *gives a picture of those who always have the sure conviction that God is present to them at all times in all places whatever they are doing. But as the Rule is here chiefly concerned with humility, it stresses the element of our sinfulness and God as judge. The frame of mind is that of the publican, praying in the Temple, "I am a sinful man, O Lord". But the Rule in these last steps is not only attentive to the inward disposition, it is also emphasizing the outward expression of it: the downcast eye, the humble bearing. All this "show" must be derived from a real conviction of one's worthlessness or else it is hypocrisy.*

The order in the Rule is from the interior of a person to the outward expression. An actor could put on an outward show without any interior motivation. These outward manifestations are better left to the instinct than done on purpose.

After all these self-conscious aspects of humility the Rule suddenly bursts out in a song of love, like a person climbing through a jungle to discover the glorious sunlight of high savannah. After climbing up all these slopes the monk will quickly arrive at that perfect love of God which casts out fear. Through this love all that he once performed with dread, he will now begin to observe . . . "no longer for fear of hell, but for love of Christ and from good habit and delight in virtue"(v. 69).

From this height, of understanding if not of achievement, perhaps we should consider the climb we have made as a whole. Remember, it is a climb down; the self has slowly and painfully been demoted, denuded of all its self-importance, which in fact did not ever have any importance. Now it could fly on the wings of the Spirit. It was all make-belief. Back to God, the giver and maker and doer of all! Away with self-importance, away with self-depending, with self. As the sequence in the Mass of Pentecost reminds us, "Nothing pure in man could be, Nothing harmless, nothing good." Yet the mystery of our faith is that in this "nothingness" can be found the Lord God himself. By his mercy and action our nothingness, once cleansed of sin and vice by the Holy Spirit, can be reformed and renewed and his very life will be our life. Even though all this is God's initiative we still have our part to play. Each one of us is a co-worker with God.* But as the Rule says it will now be a work of love.

8. On the Divine Office at Night

February 10
June 11
October 11

[1]In winter, that is, from the 1st November until Easter, it seems sensible to get up at the eighth hour of the night, [2]so that by sleeping a little beyond midnight, the brethren may rise with their food fully digested. [3]The time remaining after

---

*The relationship in our salvation between the activity of God himself and our activity has surfaced again in our time. Is it all God's work? Do we simply have to "relax", "let go" as the saying is or are we too workmen working at our salvation? The best statements have been made in two great Councils: Trent and Vatican II; Trent in the section on Justification; Vatican II in the "Constitution on the Church" (*Lumen Gentium*) chapter IV, 39–42, but particularly 40 paras 2 and 3.

Vigils should be devoted to the study of the psalter or lessons by those brethren who need to know them better.

[4]From Easter until the 1st November, as mentioned above, the hour of rising should be adjusted to allow a very short interval after Vigils during which the brethren may attend to the needs of nature. Lauds should follow straight-away, at first light.

This chapter, which deals with the times of Matins (called Vigils here) during the summer or the winter months, in fact seems more concerned with the human needs of the monks. St Benedict's aim is that the monks should have enough sleep for their digestive systems to work and for them to have time to relieve themselves. But he is also aware of the tendency we almost all have to waste time, and so, when there is space between Matins and Lauds, let that be occupied, he says, with learning the psalms or with good reading.

Brother Body to him is not an enemy to be chastised mercilessly, but a companion in the journey to heaven, to be cherished but not spoilt.

He takes the Church's fasts for granted and adds some more; he forbids meat of four-footed animals – he does not apparently therefore forbid the flesh of birds – but in this he was not going further than the frugal way the ordinary people of the time lived.

The ancient Rule tried to "cover" day and night with the praises of God. The time of Vigils or Matins should find the monks praising the Lord, awaiting the dawn; as the light comes in the eastern sky once again the monks should salute the sun, symbol of Christ, the Sun of Justice, the Lord of the New Day. St Benedict was no exception.

9. The Number of Psalms to Be Said at the Night Office

Ps. 50(51):17

[1]In winter, as mentioned above, the versicle, "Lord, open my lips and my mouth shall declare your praise" should first be repeated three times. [2]Next should come Psalm 3, with "Glory be to the Father"; [3]Psalm 94 with an antiphon, or at least chanted; [4]then an ambrosian hymn, followed by six psalms with antiphons.

[5]After the psalmody, a versicle should be said and the abbot give a blessing. Then, when all are seated in their places, three lessons from the book on the lectern should be read by the brethren in turn. Three responsories are to be chanted between them, [6]two without "Glory be to the Father"; after the third lesson, however, the reader should chant "Glory be to the Father." [7]As soon as he has begun, all are to rise from their seats out of honour and reverence for the Blessed Trinity.

[8]The books to be read at Vigils should include not only the inspired scriptures of the Old and New Testaments, but also the commentaries on them by esteemed and orthodox Catholic Fathers.

[9]After these three lessons and responsories, the remaining six psalms are to be sung with "alleluia". [10]After them should follow a lesson from the apostle, recited by heart, a versicle and the litany, that is, "Lord, have mercy"; [11]and so ends Vigils.

"Lord, open my lips . . .", like "O God come to my assistance . . ." is a beautiful sentence for pondering. In fact here we are told to repeat it three times. Why three? In honour of the Holy Trinity. The early Church, the Church of the Roman Empire, was the time God chose to unfold the stupendous revelation of the divine nature; three in One, as it had been first disclosed, so gradually and discreetly by Jesus. But by the time of St Benedict, and for some centuries before, it was the central theme of the Christian spirit. Consequently everything was made or done three-fold, from Patrick's shamrock, to the triple singing of this versicle. At the end of every psalm of the office the praise of the Three Persons was sung; so too the ending of the hymns and of the prayers would have a statement of this greatest of mysteries.

These early founders of our liturgies of the East and West were not merely emphasizing a doctrine of the Catholic Church but drawing our minds and hearts back into the dazzling darkness of the supreme Being, the Godhead whom we would worship and love with all our hearts. The Fathers of the early Church were proclaiming a fact, the fact of the Trinity; not merely three aspects of one God but a personal threefold relationship in the Godhead: Father, Son, Spirit.

The Church, after the huge energy demanded of it to hold and establish that complex mystery, being "caught" in the terminology of Greece, seems to have said instinctively: that is enough, let us leave further explanation to later times.

Today we accept all that and the massive synthesis of St Thomas Aquinas. But have we lost the excitement of the discovery?

Every reality we glimpse at within God is infinite, embracing all the rest; everything of God done in creation is done by All-God. Yet the Father is not the Son, nor the Son the Father; neither is the Spirit the Father or the Son, nor they the Spirit of both or either. Three in One, One in Three. The fundamental difference is the relationship between them, and that is infinite too.

Perhaps the Lord has let us know all this for two main reasons: (1) to make the method of our redemption more intelligible to us: (2) to give us the beginning of a realization of life within the Godhead. God is not wood or stone but infinitely alive.

Besides, it is this life within the Holy Trinity which we already share now on earth in some measure and will share in all our capacity in heaven by God's infinite mercy.

The Prayer of the Church. *An increasing number of the People of God are returning to the Prayer of the Church, the* Opus Dei, *the work of God, the liturgy of the hours, in order to enrich their prayer, to experience a fellowship with the whole church in its prayer life, to discover the beauty and wonder of the breviary, the book made up of the ancient prayers of the Hebrew people – Jesus' own people – in the Psalms, to feed on those especially chosen passages from God's own word, sacred scripture, to learn about the Father, Jesus and the Spirit from the writings of the Saints and other holy writers.*

It would be difficult to find a more spiritually profound anthology of holy readings than this one, gathered in the Prayer of the Church.

The Psalms present some problems, which arise partly from our inadequate grasp of the contents of the Old Testament. In the first place we must remember God's intimate dealings with the Jews and the Patriarchs, going back nearly two thousand years before Christ. God was forever weaning them from false ways. These barbaric ways sometimes emerge like ancient strata of rocks in a landscape, gigantic and crude.

We are not expected to share in the bloodthirsty outcries of these writers of thousands of years ago, but rather to marvel at the glorious contrast of Christ's attitude to his persecutors, showing this unique virtue of compassion, of forgiveness, magnanimity, love of enemies.

Some of these brutal psalms have been omitted in the Church's new Prayer of the Church. *Some feel that this is a pity. We are happy to follow the wisdom of the Church's leaders. Truly they are part of holy scripture, but some parts are more helpful to prayer than others. Genealogies, for instance, mostly do not readily help prayer either.*

These "cursing" psalms apart, the hymns and spiritual canticles have an objectivity, a realism, a wide span of human emotions, from the despairing cry of the soul in agony to the ecstatic joy of a human heart swept up in the divine embrace, from deepest sorrow for sin to deepest gratitude for all God's goodness to us. Underlying the personal prayers emerges the promise of salvation, of the Messiah and the mysterious premonitions of the passion; the King, yes, but one despised by men.

Jesus often used the psalms and St Benedict quotes them in his Rule more than any other book of the Bible.

10. How the Night Office Is to Be Performed in Summer

February 12
June 13
October 13

[1]From Easter until the 1st November, the number of psalms should be exactly as given above, [2]but the lessons from the book should be omitted as the nights are shorter.

In place of the three lessons, there is to be one from the Old Testament, said by heart and followed by a short responsory. [3]Everything else is to be done as stipulated. That is to say, there should never be fewer than twelve psalms at Vigils, not counting Psalms 3 and 94.

You would expect that because the nights are shorter there would be more time for reading, not less, and therefore no need to omit these readings. But what St Benedict is calculating is the lessening of the time between Matins and Lauds which follows at daybreak. He does not want Lauds to follow immediately on Matins, with the inevitable sense of rush, time becoming our master not our servant.

11. How Vigils Is to Be Performed on Sundays

February 13
June 14
October 14

[1]On Sundays all should rise earlier for Vigils, [2]which should be of the proper length. That is to say, after six psalms and a versicle have been recited as enjoined above, and all are seated in their stalls in the proper order, there should be four lessons from the book, together with their responsories, as mentioned earlier. [3]Only in the fourth responsory should the reader chant "Glory be to the Father." As soon as he begins it, all are to rise out of reverence.

[4]After these lessons another six psalms should follow in order, with antiphons as before; then a versicle; [5]and another four lessons with responsories, as above. [6]Then, three canticles from the prophets, chosen by the abbot, are to be chanted with "alleluia". [7]After the versicle and the abbot's blessing, four more lessons from the New Testament should be read, in the same way as before.

[8]After the fourth responsory, the abbot should intone the hymn *Te Deum laudamus* ("We praise you, O God"). [9]When it is finished, he is to read the lesson from the gospels while all stand in reverence and awe. [10]At the end of the reading, all are to respond, "Amen". The abbot should next intone the hymn *Te decet Laus* ("To you be praise"); and after the blessing, Lauds should begin.

[11]This arrangement for Sunday Vigils should be followed at all times, both

summer and winter, [12]unless – God
forbid – they happen to get up late. In
that case, the lessons or responsories will
have to be shortened. [13]Great care must
be taken that this should not happen; but
if it does, the one at fault is to make due
satisfaction to God in the oratory.

*Sunday has longer Matins and so the Rule demands that it be
begun somewhat earlier. Lauds, apart from the traditional*
Miserere *(Ps. 50), is full of joy and praise of the Lord in memory
of the Resurrection of Christ our Lord, each Sunday being
another Easter Day and reflecting the glory of that Day of days.*

*We can easily overlook the important emphasis in the Rule
upon Easter. Even Lent, which we tend to take rather
lugubriously, is taken in the Rule with joy, as it looks forward to
and is a preparation for the great feast of the Pasch or Easter,
feast of the death and resurrection of Jesus the Lord.*

Two most ancient hymns are included in Sunday Matins: The
Te Deum *intoned by the Abbot, and still known to all; the other,
sung after the Gospel, the* Te decet Laus, *("To you be praise"),
less well-known, is no less beautiful.*

*The end of chapter 11 is very typical of the Rule in its
considerateness. If the monks over-sleep, that of course is
regrettable, but even so St Benedict does not want to add to the
dislocations, but, keeping exactly to the prayers laid down, he
says: "the lessons or responsories will have to be shortened." So
likewise, an over-busy housewife or husband home from excess of
work is not expected to do the impossible. Their prayers must be
cut in quantity. So many happenings can dislocate the timetable
of those living and working in the world.*

12. How the Solemnity of Lauds Is to Be Performed

February 14
June 15
October 15

[1]Lauds on Sunday should begin with Psalm 66, said straight through without an antiphon. [2]After that, Psalm 50 should be said with "alleluia", [3]then Psalms 117 and 62; [4]the canticle of the Three Young Men should come next, with the psalms of praise (148 – 150), a lesson from the Apocalypse recited by heart, a responsory, ambrosian hymn, versicle, gospel canticle, litany; and so ends Lauds.

Interesting that Sunday Lauds should, though an "hour" of praise, always include the Miserere, *to remind us of our misery, our sinfulness, need for forgiveness, and also of God's endless loving kindness.*

13. How Lauds Is to Be Performed on Ordinary Week-Days

February 15
June 16
October 16

[1]On ordinary week-days, Lauds should be celebrated as follows: [2]first, Psalm 66 should be said without an antiphon and a little slowly, as on Sunday, so that everyone may assemble in time for Psalm 50, said with an antiphon. [3]Then two other psalms are to be said, according to custom: [4]on Monday, Psalms 5 and 35; [5]on Tuesday, 42 and 56; [6]on Wednesday, 63 and 64; [7]on Thursday, 87 and 89; [8]on Friday, 75 and 91; [9]and on Saturday, Psalm 142 and the canticle from Deuteronomy, divided into two parts, with "Glory be to the Father" after each. [10] On

other days, however, there is to be a canticle from the prophets proper to the day, chanted according to the custom of the Roman church. [11]Afterwards should come the psalms of praise (148 – 150), a lesson from the apostle recited by heart, a responsory, ambrosian hymn, versicle, gospel canticle, litany and conclusion.

February 16
June 17
October 17

[12]Of course, the offices of Lauds and Vespers ought never to end without the superior finally reciting, for all to hear, the whole of the Lord's prayer, on account of the thorns of contention that frequently spring up. [13]Warned as they are by the covenant made in the words of *Matt. 6:12* that prayer, "forgive us as we forgive", may they themselves be cleansed of such faults. [14]At the other offices, only the last part of the prayer is to be said aloud, in *Matt. 6:13* order that all may respond, "But deliver us from evil."

It begins in a matter of fact way, with lists of psalms and canticles. Its ending however, is special, dealing with a unique way of reciting the Our Father. Every "hour" includes the saying of the Lord's prayer, but in silence except for the ending. Here at Lauds it is all to be recited aloud in order to remind the brethren that God will forgive our sins only provided we have forgiven one another, showing what great importance St Benedict gives to the second commandment, that of loving one another, especially after any upset. He himself is most concerned not to disturb the peace of the brethren by fussy legalism, as we have just seen in chapter 12 where instead of keeping to the "letter of the law" of saying every piece of the Divine Office, he says: No, as we are late, then shorten this and that. There are plenty of other examples of his concern: for instance, providing help to a monk who is over-worked.

14. How Vigils Is to Be Performed on Saints' Days

February 17
June 18
October 18

[1]On the feasts of saints, and indeed all festivals, the office is to be performed as we have laid down for Sundays, [2]except that the psalms, antiphons and lessons proper to the day are to be said. The general arrangement, however, is to be as described above.

Saints are not much mentioned in the Rule, though occasionally obscure lives of saints are quoted. And when saints are mentioned, it may be only a reference to their relics which lie under the altar in the Church. The greatest of all the saints, Mary the Mother of God, is never mentioned at all. That does not mean there was neglect of the saints, but simply no opportunity for mention occurred, and for St Benedict the great feast was Easter, the resurrection of the Holy One of Israel.

15. The Seasons at Which Alleluia Is to Be Said

February 18
June 19
October 19

[1]From the holy feast of Easter until Pentecost, "alleluia" is always to be said with both psalms and responsories. [2]From Pentecost until the beginning of Lent, it is to be said every night with the last six psalms of Vigils only. [3]On every Sunday outside Lent, "alleluia" is to be said with the canticles of Vigils, and at Lauds, Prime, Terce, Sext and None. Vespers, however, should have an antiphon. [4]Responsories are never to be said with "alleluia", except from Easter to Pentecost.

All this excitement over the use of the "alleluia" is really excitement about the overall feast of Easter to Pentecost; and for good measure every Sunday of the year is to have a similar "alleluia" treatment, because of course every Sunday is a reminder of the resurrection, just as Easter is.

The remembrance of Christ's resurrection was not simply a reminder that Jesus himself had risen from the dead, nor just part of the apologetic for believing in the divinity of Christ, as he had foretold he would overcome death, but perhaps even more a reminder to us and all the world that we too, all of us, will rise again on the last day, bodies transformed into his. As we in baptism have died with him, so we shall rise with him on the last day.

"Alleluia", a Hebrew word, common in the Psalter, means "Praise (be to) God". It is good that in the Roman and monastic liturgy we have preserved a few Hebrew words, such as Alleluia, Amen, and Maranatha (though this is Aramaic). and Greek words like, Kyrie eleison. They remind us of our roots in Jewish and Greek civilizations. Many of the very earliest converts were Greek-speaking. All the New Testament has come down to us only in Greek.

February 19 **June 20** **October 20**	## 16. How the Work of God Is to Be Performed During the Day

Ps. 118(119):164 [1]As the prophet says, "Seven times a day have I given you praise." [2]This sacred number of seven will be fulfilled by us if we discharge our duty of service in Lauds, Prime, Terce, Sext, None, Vespers and Compline; [3]for it was of

Ps. 118(119):164 these day hours that he said, "Seven times a day have I given you praise." [4]Concerning Vigils, the same prophet

Ps. 118(119):62 says, "At midnight I arose to give you praise." [5]Consequently, we ought to praise our Creator for his just decrees at

cf Ps. 118(119):62   these times: Lauds, Prime, Terce, Sext,
None, Vespers and Compline; and let us
rise at night to give him praise.

*Seven times a day, the monks prayed and pray, and once in the
night. It is typical that the practice should spring from or be
linked with the sentence of Psalm 118 (119) verse 164, typical
because there is no other definite reason for* seven times. *The idea
in the psalm is probably to remind us we should pray* always,
*and, by making public prayer seven times a day, the Rule is
reminding us all, lay people as well as monks, that all the day
should be impregnated, perfumed with the presence of God. The
monks of the desert had this as one of their primary objectives in
going to the desert: how to pray always; St Benedict also.*

17. The Number of Psalms to Be Sung at these Hours

February 20   [1]We have already settled the order of
June 21   psalmody for Vigils and Lauds. Now we
October 21   must look at the remaining hours.
    [2]At Prime three psalms are to be said,
one by one, and not under the same
"Glory be to the Father"; [3]the hymn
proper to the hour should come after the
Ps. 69(70):2   versicle, "O God, come to my assistance", before the psalms begin. [4]When
the three psalms are finished, a single
lesson should be recited, than a versicle,
"Lord, have mercy", and conclusion.
[5]Prayer at Terce, Sext and None should
be celebrated in the same way: that is,

versicle, hymn for the hour, three psalms, lesson, versicle, "Lord have mercy", and conclusion. [6]In a larger community, the psalms should have antiphons; in a smaller one, they should be sung without.

[7]The service of Vespers is to consist of four psalms with antiphons. [8]A lesson is to be recited after the psalms, then come the responsory, ambrosian hymn, versicle, gospel canticle, litany, and to end, the Lord's prayer. [9]Compline should be limited to the saying of three psalms, said straight through without antiphons. [10]After them come the hymn for the hour, a single lesson, versicle, "Lord, have mercy", and to end, the blessing.

Nothing remarkable except for liturgical experts who will notice four psalms, not five as in the old Roman Breviary. But important is the mention of the "gospel canticle". No mention is made of which canticle it is or which Gospel, but all knew it was the Magnificat. So here we have Benedict's reverence for Mary though her name is not mentioned: her song every day of the year – her song of humility and gratitude to God, of truthfulness, of littleness, of trust.

Compline in the Rule is exceedingly short, a real "last thing" before bed; three psalms, no antiphons, and straight through; then the hymn for the hour, a reading, a versicle, "Lord have mercy", a blessing, the dismissal – no mention of the Salve Regina, yet. It had not been composed.

18. The Order in Which the Psalms are to be Said

February 21
June 22
October 22

Ps. 69(70):2

[1]First of all should be said the versicle, "O God, come to my assistance; Lord, make haste to help me" and "Glory be to the Father"; then the hymn proper to the hour.

[2]Then, at Prime on Sunday, four sections of Psalm 118 are to be said; [3]and at the rest of the hours, that is, Terce, Sext and None, three more sections of the same Psalm 118. [4]At Prime on Monday, three psalms are to be said: namely, 1, 2 and 6; [5]and similarly at Prime every day until Sunday, three psalms are to be said in order up to Psalm 19, but with Psalms 9 and 17 divided into two. [6]In this way, Vigils on Sunday will always begin with Psalm 20.

February 22
June 23
October 23

[7]At Terce, Sext and None on Monday, the remaining nine sections of Psalm 118 are to be said, three at each hour. [8]Psalm 118 having thus been said in two days, Sunday and Monday, [9]at Terce, Sext and None on Tuesday, three psalms are to be recited, from 119 to 127, making nine psalms. [10]These should be repeated at the same hours every day until Sunday. Similarly, the arrangement of hymns, lessons and versicles should be the same every day. [11]Thus, Psalm 118 will always begin on Sunday.

February 23
June 24
October 24

[12]At Vespers, four psalms are to be sung every day, [13]beginning with Psalm

109 and ending with Psalm 147, [14]but omitting those assigned to other hours, namely, Psalms 117 to 127 and Psalms 133 and 142. [15]All the rest are to be said at Vespers; [16]and as there are three psalms too few, the longer psalms in the above group are to be divided: that is, Psalms 138, 143 and 144. [17]But as Psalm 116 is short, it should be joined to Psalm 115. [18]The order of the Vesper psalms being thus settled, the remainder – lesson, responsory, hymn, versicle and canticle – is to be carried out as laid down above. [19]At Compline, the same psalms are to be said every day, namely, 4, 90 and 133.

February 24 (Leap Year only) June 25 October 25

[20]The order of psalmody for the day hours being fixed in this manner, all the remaining psalms are to be evenly distributed among the seven offices of Vigils [21]by dividing the longer ones and assigning twelve psalms to each night.

[22]Above all, we stress that if anyone finds this arrangement of the psalms unsatisfactory, he should rearrange them in whatever way he judges better, [23]provided that every care be taken that the psalter with its full complement of one hundred and fifty psalms should be chanted every week, beginning afresh every Sunday at Vigils. [24]Monks who sing less than the whole psalter and customary canticles in the course of a week show extreme slackness and lack of devotion in their service. [25]We do, indeed, read that our holy fathers in their zeal carried out in a single day what I trust we lukewarm people may accomplish in a whole week.

All the day hours begin "O God come to my assistance, Lord make haste to help me". This is perhaps the oldest monastic "word", like the Jesus Prayer which is associated with the monks of Mount Athos: that is, a word, a phrase or sentence which these holy men and women of the desert would repeat endlessly like the tolling of a deep bell, words so full of meaning as never to fail. This particular one has the tremendous Christian truth that we cannot save ourselves. The God-life is a gift beyond all gifts, beyond all natural hopes and all natural endeavour. And yet we have to do our part: "Come to my assistance".

Verses 22–25 are a very typical St Benedict comment. He not merely allows that others might disagree with him in his careful arrangement of psalms, he stresses that those who do not agree should not hesitate to arrange them in the way they prefer. He even gives this a top priority. The Rule is for monks, not monks for the Rule. The Sabbath was made for man, not man for the Sabbath.

He makes one proviso: that whatever arrangement is made, at least his monks will say the 150 psalms in a week, anything else would show "extreme slackness", so he says. It is a curious fact that the Rule as it stands has the monks saying over 220 psalms a week, by considerable repetition, such as of the Miserere, Psalm 94 and so on every day. Modern monks in most monasteries have rearranged the psalter; those with little external work have kept to St Benedict's pleas of the 150 psalms in the week; others, more busy ones, recite the 150 in two weeks. Of the two, the former is closer to the tradition. Those in the world who wish to share in the Opus Dei of the monks have their own problems: how much of the Office should be said and when? Those whose time is their own could at least say the Morning Office (Lauds) and Evening Prayer (Vespers). These are after all the two major Offices of the whole daily cycle. Of course the rest could be said.

It is becoming common for monastic mission-houses or parishes to say these morning and evening prayers in public, with lay people taking part. In abbeys and priories lay people are allowed to join in, but not always in the choir.

A busy worker in the field or town, a busy housewife and mother, any busy person; a nurse or doctor, postman, fireman or clerk, all these have very limited time for set prayers such as the Divine Office and very uncertain times at which to say them. Daily Mass comes first, if that is possible. That said, what of the Divine Office? It could be very curtailed, even to a couple of psalms or even one. But the very fact of reciting just that could be a special experience of sharing in the Opus Dei *of the monks. By joining in the prayer of the monks in the* Morning and Evening Prayer, *with their hymns, psalms and readings, with their New Testament canticles, – the* Benedictus and Magnificat – *and the final prayer, they are sharing in the Prayer of the whole Church everywhere, something that has gone on for centuries. In the world where lay people co-operate in keeping God's creative work, God's world-work – that wider* Opus Dei – *in operation, they do not have all the time the monks have to give their minds to conscious praise of God in community or even private prayer.*

Yet there is no doubt that many lay people are conscious, joyfully conscious in their every occupation, of God's living presence, and that by doing their job, their "work", they recognize that they are helping in God's work, a fundamental Opus Dei, *the divine work of God's continuing creativity. Prayer is the expressed awareness of this manifold union with God, especially so the Divine Office, the Prayer of the Church.*

19. On the Discipline of Singing the Psalms

February 24/25
June 26
October 26

Prov. 15:3

[1]We believe that God's presence is everywhere, and that "In every place the eyes of the Lord are watching the good and the bad." [2]Especially ought we to believe this, without the slightest doubt, when we are celebrating the divine office. [3]Let us always be mindful, there-

Ps. 2:11; fore, of what the prophet says, "Serve

Ps. 46(47):8;
Ps. 137 (138):1

the Lord with fear" [4]and again, "Sing wisely", [5]and,"In the sight of the angels I will sing to you."

[6]Let us consider, then, how we ought to behave in the presence of God and his angels, [7]and stand and sing the psalms in such a way that our mind and voice may be in harmony.

The "discipline" in the chapter title means "the discipline of mind and heart during the recitation or singing of the psalms"; perhaps quite simply the manner or best way of praying the psalms. St Benedict goes straight to the point: words are no use if we are not aware that God is listening. God is present everywhere, always but particularly when we are talking with him. I am amazed and horrified at myself, talking with God and thinking of something else, and what things! Perhaps many have this experience. So the Rule goes on, quoting Psalm 2:11, "Serve the Lord with fear": a reverential, respectful, loving fear. When we "say our prayers" it is wise not to rush into them but rather first to consider carefully who is listening.

20. On Reverence in Prayer

February 25/26
June 27
October 27

[1]Whenever we want to ask something from powerful people, we do not presume to do so without humility and respect. [2]How much more ought we to pray to the Lord God of all things with profound humility and pure devotion! [3]And we must realize that we shall be heard not for our many words, but for our purity of heart and tears of compunction. [4]Prayer, therefore, ought always to be short and pure, unless perhaps prolonged by the inspiration of God's

grace. [5]In community, however, prayer should be kept very short; and as soon as the signal has been given by the superior, all should rise together.

This chapter follows on straight from chapter 19. We behave before a very important person with great respect; consequently with how much more respect should we appear before the majesty, the might of the infinite God. Now follows a highly concentrated little treatise on prayer, with a variant description of prayer as either, "pure devotion" (v. 2) or "purity of heart" (v. 3), along with "humility" and "respect". All of which have a long history in the theology of prayer, especially in the writing of the Fathers of the early Church. Both "purity" and "heart" have a very firm meaning in the Christian tradition: a strong action of the will, of our whole, our deepest being. The curious thing is that this is the translation for the Greek word apatheia, *commonly used in the writings of the Desert Fathers, especially Evagrius of Pontus. Its original pagan meaning was* detachment, *without feeling, a state of insensibility, coldness. The Christians took the word over from Greek use, from the Stoics and others. So in the Greek-speaking Church it was liable to be misunderstood. The primary attitude of a Christian in prayer is not non-attachment. It is a firm deep longing or attachment (love) with all our heart, mind, soul, strength and all our being, for God. John Cassian, monk of Marseilles, who brought news to the West of the multitude of God's servants in the desert, had the great wisdom, in his work on these same monks, to translate* apatheia *into purity of heart or of devotion and, something over one hundred years later, we find it enshrined in the Rule of St Benedict. Christians are neither Stoics nor Buddhists. We have a profound respect for creation as a work of God's own hand, and as a sign of God's beauty, wisdom, love and power. We do love these works of God. But above all we love God. We are not attached to the creature; we are to the Creator, with a pure heart and devotion.*

It may seem this is all exceedingly remote. But that is far from the truth because, in the West, Christian lay people are being inundated with books and pamphlets, talks and television programmes on Eastern religions, for whom, so it would seem, prayer is no more than the ancient Stoic belief of complete detachment; it is the modern version of "Quietism".

The better gurus from the Far East would certainly say this is a travesty of their teaching, and one would willingly agree. The point is that by the time it reaches John Jones and Cissy Smith the subtleties have gone and pure negation alone survives. This is the more likely as the doctrine of a distinct loving God in these sects is often absent or blurred. Christian prayer is love as well as forgetfulness of self. God is love. He wants us to love in return.

Prayer should be brief. Does the Rule mean that the time taken over it should be brief or that we should not engage in long-winded prayers? Certainly it does not encourage the latter. In the world as in the cloister those swift shafts of love toward God, which come from a grateful heart, are precious. If the spirit so disposes and we have time, then let this movement be extended, so long as the spirit urges us. These "longings" for God and for his holy will to be done persist in that state if not contradicted, even though scarcely, if at all, adverted to; they are like a pilgrim's deep-seated determination to reach his goal: Compostella, Rome, Jerusalem. Every morning he takes his staff to set off; he meets others on his way, but his face is still firmly turned towards his goal; he takes refreshment, he rests, he buys what he needs, but always as a pilgrim on his way. So we, journeying towards God, thrust forward longing to say: We have spent one more day in God's service by his loving grace and mercy, nothing deflecting us from our resolve.

St Benedict here is discussing private prayer. He says that the superior at the end of public prayer must see to it that the joint private prayer is not merely short but very short. Here undoubtedly "short" means short in time. This awareness of others in our private devotions can also apply to those living in secular surroundings and particularly in the home. Husband and wife, no matter how united they may be, may not be drawn to the same devotional practices or needs. One may like the rosary, the other the breviary; one silent meditation, the other shared prayer; one going to Mass daily, the other satisfied with the Sunday celebration. These likes should be respected. Just as important is the sharing of those precious moments – often too few – of an evening rather than withdrawing to attend to private devotions. Private devotions should not encroach on these if either feels unfairly cut off by them.

21. On the Deans of the Monastery

February 26/27
June 28
October 28

[1]If the community is comparatively large, some brethren of sound reputation and holy life should be chosen for appointment as deans. [2]They should be responsible for their deaneries in every respect, managing them in accordance with the commandments of God and the instructions of the abbot. [3]Those chosen as deans should be the kind of people with whom the abbot can confidently share his burdens. [4]They should not be chosen by rank, but according to their worthiness of life and wise teaching.

[5]If any of these deans should happen to become puffed up with pride and found deserving of blame, he is to be corrected once, twice, even a third time. If he refuses to amend, he is to be deposed [6]and someone else, worthy of it, put in his place. [7]Furthermore, we order the same to be done in the case of the prior.

St Benedict seems to have had difficulties with his subordinate superiors. The virtue he requires of deans (decani, one over each ten monks) is humility, meaning in this instance not being puffed up by having been put over others. Anyone given such a difficult job begins with diffidence, but unless he is careful – and this includes abbots themselves – he can begin to think that only he has good ideas, good methods; a kind of minor infallibilism creeps in. He resents objections put or suggestions made; he sees threats to his superiority in the gifts others may posses.

St Benedict is very gentle with deans, as he advises that one should not demote them at the first sign of pride but warn them three times. Only then, if they do not take the hint, release them of their office.

The abbot's hope however is, according to St Benedict, that he can share the burden of Rule. How lonely a leader can make himself by not daring to trust himself to others. In many areas of government he cannot and ought not to do so, as he carries the secrets and burdens of others. Besides, others who can be trusted with confidence are few indeed. This is one of the most subtle areas of leadership. We are none of us wise in all things, but by wise choice of counsellors or deans an abbot has acquired the accumulated wisdom of the Community, judiciously enquiring of now this monk now that. So too all of us in humility and prudence must seek advice. But at the end, we must decide in our own affairs.

22. How the Monks Are to Sleep

February 27/28
June 29
October 29

¹They should each sleep in a separate bed. ²They should receive bedding appropriate to the monastic way of life, as provided for by the abbot. ³If possible, all should sleep in one place; but if their numbers do not permit that, they should sleep in groups of ten or twenty, under the careful supervision of seniors. ⁴There ought to be a light burning in the room until morning.

⁵They should sleep clothed, and girded with belts or cords; but they ought not to have their knives beside them, in case

they should cut themselves in their sleep. [6]Thus, the monks will always be ready to get up without delay when the signal is given and make haste to arrive at the Work of God before the others, yet with complete dignity and propriety.

[7]The younger brethren should not have beds next to one another but mixed in among the seniors. [8]When they get up for the Work of God, let them gently encourage one another, for the sleepy are apt to make excuses.

It might be expected that, fifteen hundred years ago, monks would be sleeping on mats on the floor. Even today that would be completely normal in many parts of the world, such as India and Africa. But no, each monk is to have a bed, bedding on top of that, but only what is suitable for monks – that is, simple, not expensive; adequate, not luxurious, but let the abbot decide. That seems to be the drift; once again, no exaggeration either way: nothing extravagant, nor, on the other hand, something inadequate, which fails to keep the shivering monk warm. The parallel we are looking for here is easily visible. He would want us all to have what is normal for our station in life, but nothing lavish, absurdly expensive, just for show.

Perhaps we should be more concerned with the wages of those who provide us with all we need, from miners to dress-makers, from men and women on the coffee plantations and those who put lids on boxes, than with the cost to us of our clothes.

The Rule is aiming that all should go to bed at the same hour and in the same dormitory; this will more surely make for all rising together. Regular hours are a considerable aid to peace of mind.

Children together, uncontrolled, get up to all kinds of mischief, harmless or harmful. Yet St Benedict has the humanity to encourage them to urge each other, not boisterously, to rise in the morning.

23. On Excommunication for Faults

February 28/29
June 30
October 30

[1]If any brother is found to be insubordinate or disobedient or proud, or if he is a grumbler or in any way despises the holy Rule and shows contempt for the orders of his seniors, [2]he should twice be warned privately by the seniors, in accordance with our Lord's precept. [3]If he does not amend, he is to be rebuked publicly, in front of everyone. [4]If even then, however, he does not reform, he is to be excommunicated, provided that he understands the nature of his punishment. [5]But if he will not understand, he should undergo corporal punishment.

cf Matt. 18:15–16

24. What the Measure of Excommunication Should Be

March 1
July 1
October 31

[1]The measure of excommunication or punishment should be in proportion to the seriousness of the fault, [2]which it is for the abbot to determine.

[3]If a brother is found guilty of less serious faults, he is to be excluded from sharing the common table. [4]This is to be the rule for anyone excluded from the common table: in the oratory he is not to intone psalm or antiphon, nor recite a lesson, until satisfaction has been made. [5]He is to have his meals alone, after the brethren have eaten. [6]So if, for instance, the brethren eat at the sixth hour, he is to eat at the ninth; if they eat at the ninth hour, he is to eat in the evening, [7]until by appropriate satisfaction he may obtain pardon.

25. *On More Serious Faults*

March 2
July 2
November 1

[1]The brother who is guilty of a more serious fault is to be excluded from both the table and the oratory. [2]None of the brethren should associate with him or talk to him at all. [3]He is to work alone at the task assigned to him and remain in sorrow and penance as he ponders that

1 Cor. 5:5 fearful sentence of the apostle, [4]"Such a one is handed over for the destruction of his flesh, that his spirit may be saved on the day of the Lord." [5]He is to have his meals alone, in the measure and at the time the abbot deems appropriate for him. [6]He is not to be blessed by anyone passing by, nor is the food given him to be blessed.

26. *On Those Who Associate with the Excommunicated Without Permission*

March 3
July 3
November 2

[1]If any brother, without the abbot's permission, presumes to associate in any way with an excommunicated brother, either talking to him or sending him a message, [2]he is to receive the same punishment of excommunication.

27. How the Abbot Must Have Special Care for the Excommunicated

Matt. 9:12

[1]The abbot must take great pains in his care for brethren who go astray, for "it is not those who are well who need a physician, but those who are sick." [2]Like a wise physician, therefore, he ought to use every means he can, sending in *senpectae*, that is, experienced and wise brethren, [3]who may, as it were, secretly comfort the faltering brother and urge him to humble himself by way of satisfaction, encouraging him, "that he may not be overwhelmed by excessive sorrow." [4]As the apostle also says, "Let love for him be reaffirmed"; and let everyone pray for him.

2 Cor. 2:7

2 Cor. 2:8

[5]The abbot must exercise the very greatest care, use all discernment and make every effort not to lose any of the sheep entrusted to him. [6]He should realize that he has undertaken responsibility for weak souls, not tyranny over strong ones. [7]Let him also fear the prophet's threat, in which God says, "What you saw to be fat, you took for yourself; and what was weak, you cast away." [8]Let him imitate the loving example of the Good Shepherd who left the ninety-nine sheep in the mountains and went in search of the one sheep that had strayed, [9]and had such great compassion on its weakness that he deigned to place it on his own sacred shoulders and so brought it back to the flock.

Ezek. 34:3-4

cf Luke 15:4-5

28. *On Those Who, though Often Corrected, Refuse to Amend*

March 5
July 5
November 4

[1] If any brother has been frequently reproved for some fault or even excommunicated, yet does not amend, he is to receive more severe correction. That is to say, he is to be punished with the rod. [2] But if he still will not amend or perhaps – God forbid – becomes puffed up with pride and takes to defending his conduct, then the abbot must act as a prudent physician would.

[3] After he has applied poultices, the ointment of encouragement, the medicine of holy scripture, and last of all, the searing iron of excommunication and strokes of the rod, [4] if then he sees that all his exertion has been to no purpose, he is to make use of something greater still, his prayers and the prayers of all the brethren, [5] that the Lord, who can do all things, may heal the ailing brother.

[6] Yet if, even in this way, he is not healed, the abbot must use the knife of amputation. As the apostle says, "Banish the evil-doer from your midst"; [7] and again, "If the unbeliever departs, let him depart", [8] lest one diseased sheep infect the whole flock.

1 Cor. 5:13

1 Cor. 7:15

29. *Whether Brethren Who Leave the Monastery Should Be Readmitted*

[1]If a brother who leaves the monastery through his own fault later wishes to return, he must first promise to make full amends for having left. [2]Then he should be readmitted to the lowest place, as a test of his humility.

[3]If he leaves again, or a third time, he should be readmitted in the same way; but after that, he must understand that all possibility of return is denied him.

30. *On the Way in Which Children Are to Be Corrected*

[1]Every age and level of understanding should receive appropriate treatment. [2]Therefore, whenever children or adolescents or those less capable of understanding the gravity of the penalty of excommunication [3]are guilty of misdemeanours, they should be disciplined with severe fasts or punished with sharp strokes, in order that they may be healed.

These chapters face up to the fact that the cowl does not make the monk. A man enters a monastery with all his faults and with the burden of Original Sin. It is the job of his lifetime, with the help of God, to recover well-being. Backsliding is inevitable. These chapters attempt to deal with this problem.

The examples of backsliding given are: obstinacy, disobedience, pride, murmuring, habitual Rule-breaking, contemptuousness of authority. They are all related, in the Rule, to obedience.

St Benedict's aim throughout these chapters is to bring back to his senses the monk who has fallen away. The approach is graded to make it easy for the disobedient to come back into line (ch. 23); first a private warning, not just once but twice; only then done publicly. If that has no effect then excommunication, but not if that kind of penalty means nothing to the erring brother; for such a one corporal punishment as a last resort – not the kind of thing at all possible in our age of violence.

Chapters 24–26: *This excommunication has in itself degrees of severity. St Benedict is not dealing with excommunication for heresy but for indiscipline, disobedience to the Rule; so, for lesser faults lesser excommunications. These are degrees of separation from the community; from sharing in the community meals (24:4), from taking a prominent part in the Divine Office, or, more grievously, being excluded from associating with the brethren (25:2), and from community meals and office. Nor must he be allowed to share in the common work, to have a blessing from all who pass, or to have his food blessed. He must live alone and anyone daring to break through this isolation of the brother will himself be excommunicated.*

Chapter 27: *However, in the background, the abbot is to send trusty monks who will secretly console the brother and persuade him not to be overwhelmed by excessive sorrow but rather to be humble and say he is sorry for his offence. The abbot is here compared to a doctor and therefore by implication the brother to a sick person. The aim of the abbot is not to crush but to save.*

The abbot is compared with the Good Shepherd who seeks out the lost sheep.

Chapter 28: *The Rule here reiterates the various efforts to bring the stray monk to his senses. But the point finally comes where nothing more can be done and in the imagery of medicine proposes that the monk be excised from the body of the community. These chapters are an object lesson in careful treatment, from persuasion to the final expulsion.*

Chapter 29: *By the stage reached in chapter 28, of the monk being expelled from the monastery, one might expect St Benedict to feel well rid of the unruly monk. But he still longs for his return. If he comes back, he must be received, if he is ready to admit his sin and be sorry, if he is prepared to take the lowest place. But more amazing still, St Benedict imagines this unruly monk fleeing the monastery not once more, but twice more. Still, if repentant and he returns, the prodigal should be accepted. After that, NO. This is an example of mercy over justice from which we can all learn.*

Chapter 30: *Boys. Someone has pointed out that no one legislates just for a few. If St Benedict lays down rules for boys, there must have been a school. We do not find fathers of a family writing a code of punishment for their children. The basis is respect, trust and love, a tradition of command and obedience. Don Bosco laid down in his schools that no one should ever beat a boy. I believe today that Don Bosco is right. But so is St Benedict in this, that there must be sanctions for a rebellious boy or one who is almost completely callous; but let them not be applied in anger, because a boy will think this uncontrolled by reason, and therefore unjust. A sanction should be applied seriously and calmly.*

Today, because of the collapse of many families, because of the appalling conditions in which their lives are spent, the oppression, sense of insecurity, children even of only five and six are sometimes completely unruly. They have not found love, nor do they believe anyone does love them, and therefore they hate all in return for this neglect. Love is the only remedy. It requires heroic patience. We can find it among the Good Shepherd sisters and others who follow Christ by working with the very young.

31. On the Kind of Person the Cellarer of the Monastery Should Be

March 8
July 8
November 7

[1]As cellarer of the monastery there should be chosen from the community a wise person of mature character, who is abstemious, not greedy, not conceited, nor a trouble-maker, not offensive or lazy or wasteful, [2]but someone who is God-fearing and may be like a father to the whole community.

[3]He is to have care of everything; [4]do nothing without the abbot's order; [5]keep to his instructions; [6]not upset the brethren. [7]Should any brother chance to make an unreasonable request, he is not to upset him by snubbing him. Instead, he should refuse the unreasonable request in the proper way, with humility. [8]Let him keep guard over his own soul, always bearing in mind that saying of the apostle, "One who serves well obtains a good standing for himself."

1 Tim. 3:13

[9]He should take meticulous care of the sick, the young, guests and the poor, knowing for certain that he will have to account for them all on judgment day. [10]All the monastery's utensils and goods he should regard as if sacred altar vessels. [11]He must let nothing be neglected. [12]He should studiously avoid both miserliness and extravagant squandering of the monastery's resources, and instead do all things with moderation and in accordance with the abbot's instructions.

March 9
July 9
November 8

Sir. 18:17

Matt. 18:6

¹³Above all, he should possess humility; and when he lacks the wherewithal to meet a request, he should give a good word in answer, ¹⁴as it is written, "A good word is above the best gift." ¹⁵Everything entrusted to him by the abbot is to be under his care, but he must not presume to meddle with anything forbidden him. ¹⁶He should give the brethren their allowance of food without any haughtiness or delay, lest they be tempted to evil. He must bear in mind what scripture says someone deserves "who tempts one of these little ones to evil."

¹⁷If the community is comparatively large, he should be given assistants so that with their help he may do the work entrusted to him with serenity. ¹⁸Necessary items are to be applied for and distributed at appropriate times, ¹⁹in order that no one may be troubled or upset in the house of God.

Here is a character sketch of a person we should like to be or at least to have as a good friend. He has all the qualities of a community man; in fact as St Benedict says, he is "like a father to the whole community". The virtue he puts first is wisdom (v. 1), which is akin to prudence, deep and wide knowledge with the power to apply it to life, that is to human behaviour. He does not write "mature" by itself, which could mean old, but "of mature character". Some young monks are more mature in character than some old ones.

The cellarer has, under the abbot, control of all the material things of the monastery, their distribution according to the needs of each. Whatever a monk needs, it is to the cellarer he goes. St Benedict senses how crucial for the happiness and peace of the brethren is the way the cellarer reacts to requests; these obviously will not always be reasonable. The cellarer could answer "No" proudly, irritably, excitably, coldly, contemptuously; St Benedict wants him firm, yes, but calm and humble in explaining why he must refuse the request: "When he lacks the wherewithal to meet a request, he should give a good word". How apposite for all in authority, a father or mother, a teacher or "boss". So easily authority slips towards arrogance and tyranny.

The food for the brethren is his business. If he himself is greedy, he will be too lavish; if miserly, then too abstemious.

The cellarer is told to remember that all the property of the monastery – utensils, tools, furniture and so on – really belongs to God. Benefactors, when giving, are really giving to God; the gift must be treated as God's property. This of course is true of all the things anyone has: they are God's: God made them and only loans them for our use. We have both to be careful of them, and, if they are in excess of our needs, then give to those who have none.

St Benedict is also concerned to preserve the peace of mind of the cellarer himself. People should not pester him at all times of day or night, but at appointed times. If he is overburdened, he should be given assistance. Mothers cannot always find "helps" – God will provide. Believe this. The cellarer has considerable power in the monastery, so the Rule in its wisdom ensures that he does nothing except as the abbot has ordained.

It could be that St Benedict expected the cellarer to be elected, and in fact cellarers have so been. But it sounds most unlikely that St Benedict meant this, in view of his great fear of the cellarer's becoming a rival to the abbot. "Eligere", which comes early in the chapter, almost certainly here must mean choose. *Several times in this very chapter the cellarer is warned not to get "ideas above his station". He must always have the approval of the abbot, never take on any scheme without checking with the abbot.*

This chapter exemplifies to perfection the spirit of St Benedict, one of delicacy and firmness, a very precise, sensitive appreciation of the care one should have for human beings – accepting "difficult" people, neither crushing them nor pandering to their whims. Authority he sees as fatherhood, not, as some scholars think, in the Roman sense, but in Jesus' meaning of the word in the Gospel, the epitome of loving care.

There are very few in the world so isolated as not to have others over whom they have some authority, however little, or who have not others over them. This chapter applies aptly to fathers of families, and mothers too, to those in the services or in businesses, big or small. The qualities here given are those which we should all cultivate or aim to acquire.

32. On the Tools and Belongings of the Monastery

March 10
July 10
November 9

[1]The monastery's goods – tools, clothing or anything else – should be entrusted to brethren on whose character and conduct the abbot can rely. [2]He should give them charge of the various items as he thinks fit, to be looked after and collected again after use. [3]The abbot should keep a list of them, so that when the brethren succeed one another in the duties assigned them, he may be sure what he gives out and receives back.

[4]If anyone treats the monastery's belongings in a sloppy or careless way, he should be reproved. [5]If he does not amend, he should be subjected to the discipline of the Rule.

St Benedict is here taking care of the little things of life. We all know how things that are "nobody's" disappear – spades, spoons, screwdrivers, hammers, cups, chairs. He lived in an age of want – so do we, where millions have nothing. Our civilization is the "throw away" one, his the one of universal need. Besides, he had already said in the previous chapter (v. 10) that the belongings of the monastery should be treated like the sacred vessels of the altar, that is, belonging to God. We tend to think and act as though the whole world were ours. It all belongs to

God. God made it, and for a purpose, each bit of it. In a sense the world is for our use; you might say it is on loan. But that does not mean one third of the world – our third – should claim it as all our own. We might begin by recognizing all this as true in our own individual lives and treat all things we touch and use as precious belongings of God which he loans to us, or gives us for our use – the fields, the woods, the metals from mines, the fish and birds, animals, the very air we breathe, the seas and lakes and rivers, mountains and hills; the little things: the food we eat, the wood we burn, the water in the tap, our very clothes, all gifts from a loving Father.

33. Whether Monks Should Have Anything of Their Own

March 11
July 11
November 10

Acts 4:32

[1]It is of prime importance that this vice should be completely rooted out of the monastery. [2]No one should presume to give or receive anything without the abbot's permission, [3]nor keep anything as his own, anything whatsoever – no book, no writing tablets, no pen, absolutely nothing at all. [4]Indeed, they should not even have their own bodies or wills at their own disposal. [5]They ought, in fact, to look to the father of the monastery for all their needs; for it is not permissible for anyone to keep anything that the abbot has not given or allowed. [6]"All things should be common to all", as it is written, "Nor should anyone presume to claim anything as his own."

[7]Should anyone be caught indulging in this most wicked vice, he should be warned a first and second time. [8]If he does not amend, he must undergo punishment.

St Benedict is unusually firm and absolute about individual poverty, when he seems to be almost slack, for instance, on the subject of food and drink. "This vice should be completely rooted out" (v. 1). Nothing at all is to be one's own, not even book or (writing) tablet or pen or anything at all (without permission of the abbot), "since monks should not even have their own bodies or wills at their own disposal" (v. 4). Why?

The first and all-sufficient answer is that Jesus gave the example in life and word. He had not even a stone on which to lay his head. He said: "You wish to be perfect" (Matt. 19:21); "There is one thing you lack" (Mark 10:21); "There is still one thing you lack" (Luke 18:22). "Sell all that you own and distribute the money to the poor and you will have treasure in heaven; then, come, follow me" (Luke 12:33). "Sell your possessions and give . . . for where your treasure is, there will your heart be also".

He tells his special disciples to leave father, mother, brother, sister and all things, give to the poor and follow him, chosen for a special purpose. These are the words that led Antony into the desert and Francis to fall in love with Jesus and My Lady Poverty. They would eliminate all desire for possessions by being rid of all possessions. They chose the radical solution. So did St Benedict. But he, being a practical person, realised this could not be done as a group. He believed in group possession for monks, but individual poverty: no ownership by any monk. He could be granted use of things on need, with permission of the abbot. The community should own. This could become the Achilles heel of monasticism. It did in monasteries in St Francis of Assisi's time, and many other times as well. Moderation is always a problem, a precarious balance but eminently suitable for human and Christian living for all that.

This is not the form of holiness presented by the Church to lay people, though any individual in the lay world could accept it. Things are good, made by God for our use. The same is true of the sexual urge; it is good, made for our enjoyment. Both of these can be – and are by some – idolized, taking the place of God, holding all our attention, all our desires.

What St Benedict is telling us is to love things and people too, but within bounds. The urge for property can, like all our desires, become overpowering, possessing us rather than we them.

On the other hand, creation was made for our use, for our admiration, for our gratitude to God. St Benedict in the Rule wants us to use well what God has provided. At the same time, when speaking to a monastic community, he does not want jealousy, competitiveness; as scripture says, "to each according to his need".

In the Great Community – which is the whole world, we should also share out, and work in harmony with all so that "to each according to his need". The creation of great organizations, if set up to benefit not only the organizers but all, can be, should be, a great gift to humankind. They can be oppressive. This is where the crux has always been, from the times of the Egyptians – and others before them – to this our own time now.

This moderation is very specially applicable to people in the world, who live in the smaller community of the family. In whatever way property is owned, it is needed for the well-being of the group. How much? How spent? To own none, against your will, can lead to slavery.

It is quite impossible, evidently, to go down to particulars in this matter: family life will vary from group to group, country to country. We have to follow Jesus' teaching: not set our heart on riches, remembering the poor at the gate, not loving soft living. Remember Dives and Lazarus and their different fates (Luke 16:19–31). Remember our last judgment too.

Does one's station, position in life, have any bearing on this search for the Christian way? Jesus made no comment on women's dress or men's either. He did not tell the scribes or Pharisees, to change their robes, but to change their minds and hearts. He did comment on how their dress pointed to their arrogance and vanity (Matt. 23:5).

Jesus certainly did not say blessed are the rich. He did say how difficult it is for the rich man to enter heaven. St Benedict is taking extreme precautions: a monk should have NOTHING he could call his own. Not all are called to be monks. In all conditions of life it is possible to be holy. Some ways are of their nature more conducive to holiness; they set up a framework within which holiness should readily be attained. One might *think riches would give the rich marvellous opportunities be to generous. But history proves that it is rather the poor who help the poor.*

Possessing wealth is extremely attractive. It provides security, gives power, builds self-confidence – all three easily enemies to Christian living. It is in the long run false security, which could vanish overnight; power often creates frightening and ugly arrogance and is the cause of monstrous injustices. The self-confidence that comes from power is based not on real worth, virtue, real achievement, but on something external to ourselves, even if produced by our own energy and skill. God gave these too, so we should rather thank God for giving us that energy, that skill, not preen ourselves on borrowed feathers. Simplicity of life, frugality, are the hallmark of a true Christian.

34. Whether All Should Receive Necessary Items in Equal Measure

March 12
July 12
November 11

Acts 4:35

[1]As it is written, "Distribution was made to each according to need." [2]By this, we do not mean that there should be favouritism – God forbid – but rather consideration for weaknesses. [3]Whoever needs less should thank God and not be downcast. [4]Whoever needs more should be made humble because of his weakness and not give himself airs because of the kindness shown him. [5]In this way, all the members will be at peace.

[6]Above all, the wicked habit of grumbling must not show itself in any word or sign, for any reason whatever. [7]Should anyone be caught grumbling, he must be strictly punished.

In the previous chapter, St Benedict has firmly set the standard of individual poverty for monks; here he explains how that absolute denial of personal property should work out. Already he has said that monks may have for their use what they need provided that it is sanctioned by the abbot. Now he examines whether all should need exactly the same. The legally-minded legislator might lay down the same for everyone. This would be so much more convenient for the administration of the monastery, for the abbot and the cellarer; the law itself would be so much tidier. But the law is not for the sake of the law-giver or for ease of administration, as St Benedict in this chapter plainly shows; it is for the sake of those who live under it, following Jesus. **The sabbath is made for man, not man for the sabbath**.

Therefore, St Benedict lays down that each monk should be granted what he needs. That is different from what he wants, or desires.

In the modern world our desires are manipulated to make us think that what we want is what we really need. In fact we buy not what we really need or what we really want but what brewers or cigarette makers want us to want.

We can all be stimulated from outside to an irrational desire for "absolute" needs which are not needs at all. St Benedict says that those of us who require less should thank God, rather than take pride in the fact, while those who need more should be humbled by their lack of restraint. So here he is not considering absolute need, like a bandage to restore a broken arm, but a habit too difficult to break. I think his mind is turning to those who "cannot" do without wine, it would make them so distressed and disgruntled. The chapter ends with a warning against grumbling or murmuring.

We must not murmur against authority, least of all against God, against happenings beyond our control, against people. Grumblers are people who destroy the peace of a community, of a family. Grumbling is usually an expression of discontent about something or someone, but to a third party: to express this and no more, to release our feelings; it can be resentment against the person responsible. Ideally, if we feel "disaffected" about someone, the "grumble" should be made in a friendly way to that person. But, beware, do this only when the resentment has cooled. We may have a deep-seated dislike for that person, or jealousy. Our anger can be the rumbles of a not quite extinct volcano. St Benedict definitely does not like grumblers. He uses murmurare and its derivatives twelve times. He disapproves too of those who, in authority, by their thoughtless action or inaction, create a situation which causes justifiable grumbling! He himself uses this phrase in chapter 41:5.

35. On the Kitchen Servers for the Week

March 13
July 13
November 12

[1]The brethren should serve one another, with no one being excused from kitchen service except on the grounds of illness or because engaged in some important business; [2]for such service secures a richer recompense and greater love. [3]Help should be provided for the less strong, so that they may serve without distress. [4]In fact, everyone should have help as the size of the community or local conditions may require. [5]If the community is comparatively large, the cellarer should be excused kitchen service, as well as those engaged in any important business, as we said. [6]The rest should serve one another in love.

[7]On Saturday the server ending his week should do the washing. [8]He should wash the towels that the brethren use for wiping their hands and feet. [9]Then, both outgoing and incoming server should wash the feet of all. [10]The outgoing server should return the kitchen utensils, clean and in good condition, to the

cellarer, [11]who should himself then give them to the incoming server, so that he can keep a check on what he gives out or receives back.

March 14
July 14
November 13

[12]An hour before the meal, the servers for the week should receive, over and above the regular allowance, a drink and some bread, [13]in order that they may serve their brethren at mealtime without grumbling or hardship. [14]On feast days, however, they should wait until after the dismissal.

[15]On Sunday, straight after Lauds, the incoming and outgoing servers should make a profound reverence before all in the oratory and ask their prayers. [16]The server ending his week should say this

Ps. 85(86):17

verse, "Blessed are you, Lord God, who have helped me and comforted me." [17]After this has been said three times and the outgoing server has received a blessing, the incoming server should

Ps. 69(70):2

follow, saying, "O God, come to my assistance; Lord, make haste to help me." [18]Again, this should be repeated three times by all, then when he has received a blessing, the server may begin his week.

We might be disposed to criticize St Benedict in this chapter for bothering to fuss about details. We would surely be wrong. In some cases it is in the details that peace is disturbed.

In this instance everyone in the community is involved. The kitchen feeds all, the opportunities for friction are innumerable. Who should serve? How many should serve? Who is going to put things away? Who wash the feet of the brethren?

St Benedict wants everyone to take part in serving the brethren. He does not expand the reasons, except to say it is a source of grace and brings greater mutual love: the grace of humility, patience, carefulness for the sake of the brethren. But that everyone should serve and wait at table brings up the problem of monks with important jobs who would find it very difficult to spare the time – interesting that even in his monastery there might be monks so stretched for time as not to have any for waiting. Among these he singles out the cellarer. Then the sick too he excuses, not however the weak. These must be given help. It seems he does not want to deprive them of the grace and privilege of serving the brethren. Among such he would, no doubt, include the aged but not senile, because it is a joy for them to serve the brethren.

In a family there are the sick, the old, the over-burdened. One parent may be engaged all day with the little ones, the other out at work, likewise all day. By the end of the day, both are tired. Following the advice of St Benedict they should share the evening's burden lovingly, neither forgetting the other's weariness.

The underlying teaching of Jesus, which St Benedict does not express in this case, though in many others he does and implies here, is that we must see Christ in our neighbour. It applies supremely here. In a Christian family Jesus is always present.

The next paragraph is typically both practical and gracious. The last act of the outgoing kitchen servers is to imitate Jesus, in washing the feet of all the brethren, and then to hand the utensils back to the cellarer so that he knows what is in use and that it is all in good condition.

A delicate touch follows: to prevent any grumbling or weariness among the servers at the table, they should be allowed a drink* and some bread. St Benedict does not see law as something rigid, but as an aid to holiness. It is made for us. Here and elsewhere he recognizes that monks can have legitimate grievances, and the fault may, therefore, lie not with them but with the superiors. Yet they should not grumble. (The word

---

*Often translated "wine" but the latin word is *biberes*. It could mean wine here; but the point is: don't drive anyone to desperation in a matter of small consequence.

"dismissal" in verse 14 probably means "at the end of Mass".)

Finally the chapter lays down that, at the end of one week of serving and the start of another, those who are handing over should pray before the community and those beginning their week should do likewise. This is a perfect example of St Benedict's principle (see the Prologue) that when we begin anything we must do so with a prayer. But here he adds; when you complete something, pray also.

The prayers he proposes are of the kind that could be the "prayer of the day or week" like the Jesus Prayer: the first a mixture of Daniel 3:52 and Psalm 85:17, the second the prayer of the Desert Fathers which begins almost every Office "O God, come to my assistance; Lord, make haste to help me" (Ps. 69:2). The "three times" is in honour of the holy Trinity and to help it to sink in – again like the Jesus Prayer – repeated.

Every Christian serves, not just once every ten or twenty weeks, as a monk does at table or in the kitchen. In a family, father and mother are in the kitchen and at the table serving every day; in fact wherever we are, whatever we are doing, we can be serving and we would do well to remember Jesus serving at the Last Supper.

How very important to lift those humdrum elements into the world of divine action. Most have a job, in an office, a factory, in a business, school or hospital; the "job", the "work of God", of looking after one's wife or husband, the "job" or "work of God" of caring for the children. This unobtrusive chapter tucked away in the middle of the Rule has a message for all of us. It can raise the everyday into the God-world.

36. On Sick Brethren

March 15
July 15
November 14

Matt. 25:36;25:40

[1]Care of the sick must be seen to before and above everything else, so that they may truly be served as Christ himself. [2]It was he who said, "I was sick and you visited me"; [3]and, "What you did to one of these little ones, you did to me." [4]But let the sick themselves appreciate that they are being served out of reverence for God, and let them not with their excessive demands weary their brethren as they serve them. [5]All the same, the sick should be patiently borne with, because from such people a greater reward is gained. [6]The abbot, therefore, must take the utmost care that they suffer no neglect.

[7]A special room should be made available for the sick, with an attendant who is God-fearing, attentive and painstaking. [8]Baths should be allowed the sick as often as is desirable; but the healthy, and in particular the young, should be allowed them more rarely. [9]In addition, meat may be permitted to the sick who are very weak, to build up their strength; but as soon as they have recovered, all should abstain from meat as usual.

[10]The abbot must be extremely careful that the sick are not neglected by the cellarer and attendants, for he is answerable for all his disciples' shortcomings.

Here St Benedict returns straight to the gospel: the sick are Christ. Jesus said "I was sick", describing our "Last Judgment". He went on that we will be judged by our compassion for the sick, for the starving, the naked – who have NOTHING – for the dying, in fact for all those who need our help.

We are mesmerized by the images of the starving in Ethiopia or India, the catastrophes in South America, China, and feel paralyzed by the magnitude of these disasters, too big to imagine or for each, individually, to help. In fact there are organisations that do make it possible for all of us to help. The strange thing is that on the one hand we feel helpless before these and do little but suffer guilt feelings, except when the media compel us to contribute, while allowing ourselves – half unaware of doing so – to forget the many miseries on our own doorstep.

St Benedict begins "at home". There is plenty of misfortune all around us. The house-bound, the ill in hospital, the dying at home, those left behind, the very old and the almost helpless, the children abandoned or ill-treated; those in prison, the drug addicts, the alcoholics, the suicidal, the sick. The list is endless. Choose one group and come to their help, personally and financially, but personal help is the best, to those around you; then ACT. Band together, stick at it.

The second part of the chapter is written by someone who had experience. When you "dive in to help" it ceases to be idealistic theorizing: it is the business of food, the right food, baths, knowing the right agency to go to for help; it can be a matter of heating, cleaning up the mess of weeks; of listening and taking a message, just visiting and keeping it up. Once we reach a particular person, it is then that real sacrifice, real self-giving begins in earnest, and we are afraid. Pray.

But the sick can be wearisome, "with their excessive demands" (v. 4). Those who serve need patience; they may need to be strict, keeping a little restraint on the needy. Yet both those who need help and those who provide it should remember that the Lord is present in the one who serves and the one served.

37. *On the Old and the Very Young*

March 16
July 16
November 15

[1]Although human nature itself tends to be compassionate towards these ages of life, the old and the very young, the authority of the Rule should still make provision for them. [2]Their lack of strength must always be taken into account, and the strictness of the Rule as regards food should by no means apply to them. [3]On the contrary, let them be treated with sympathetic consideration and allowed to eat before the regular times.

The old have a little chapter almost all to themselves. They share it with little children. St Benedict wants compassionate care to be shown them on account of their defencelessness; and he takes for granted what underlies all the preceding chapter, that Christ must be seen in them all.

38. *On the Reader for the Week*

March 17
July 17
November 16

[1]Reading ought not to be lacking at the brethren's meals; nor ought the reader to be one who casually happens to pick up the book but someone who will read for the whole week, starting on Sunday. [2]After Mass and Communion, the incoming reader is to ask everyone to pray for him, that God may protect him from the spirit of conceit. [3]In the oratory he is to intone three times the verse, "O Lord, open my lips and my mouth shall declare your praise", which is to be

Ps. 50(51):17

repeated by all. ⁴Thus, after receiving a blessing, he is to begin reading.

⁵There should be perfect silence, with no whispering, no voice but the reader's being heard there. ⁶The brethren should serve one another whatever they require as they eat and drink, so that no one need ask for anything. ⁷However if something is wanted, it should be asked for by some kind of eloquent sign rather than by speech.

⁸No one there should presume to ask questions about the reading or anything else, lest it occasion (unruliness); ⁹but the superior may wish to say a few edifying words.

¹⁰The brother who is reader for the week should receive some light refreshment before he begins to read because of holy Communion, and in case the fast should prove hard for him to bear. ¹¹He is to have his meal afterwards, with the kitcheners and servers for the week.

¹²The brethren are not to read or sing according to rank but according to the edification they give their hearers.

We find ourselves in a well-known routine. The reader too must be chosen for the week, he must pray and ask a blessing before the start, but one new element appears. Not anyone "who casually happens to pick up the book", should be allowed to be reader, only one who can read well. It is surprising that this qualification did not occur with the cooks and servers. No one would mind not being chosen to cook, but we might be touchy about being forbidden to read unless it was there in the Rule. Not everyone in St Benedict's time was literate. Besides, the purpose of having

reading in the refectory is to benefit those who are listening; a bad
cook only causes various degrees of unease.

   We all have disabilities, physical or mental, if not in youth
then as age creeps up. Some are happy to remain in the
background, others by nature are active and competitive. Our
aim should not be to shine or to withdraw, but to help if we are
able, at least to pull our weight in our small way, or big way if
that is how God has seemingly arranged it all.

39. On the Measure of Food

March 18
July 18
November 17

[1]For the daily meal, whether at the sixth or the ninth hour, we believe that two cooked dishes for every table should be enough and allow for individual weaknesses. [2]Thus, anyone who cannot eat one kind of food may make a meal of the other. [3]Two kinds of cooked food, therefore, should be enough for all the brethren; and if any fruit or fresh vegetables are available, a third dish may be added.

[4]A full pound weight of bread should be enough for the day, whether for only one meal or for both dinner and supper. [5]If they are to have supper, a third of the pound should be set aside by the cellarer to be given to them at suppertime.

[6]If their work happens to be heavier than usual, it shall be in the abbot's power to decide whether it would be appropriate to add something. [7]Excess is to be avoided at all costs, so that a monk may never be overcome by the consequences of over-indulgence; [8]for there is

nothing so ill-becoming a Christian as excess. [9]As our Lord said, "See that your hearts are not weighed down with excess."

Luke 21:34

[10]Young children should not receive the same amount of food as their elders, but less; with frugality being observed in everything. [11]All except the sick who are very weak should abstain entirely from eating the meat of four-footed beasts.

Food is a daily problem for the provider – too much, too little, expensive, cheap. St Benedict wants enough, so that no one has grounds for grumbling, and a variety for the same reason, and points to indigestion as a sign of eating immoderately. He waxes eloquent against excess. He wants moderation.

Young boys, he claims, should be given less. We think "growing lads" require more. We must remember that in his day very small boys indeed had been handed over to the care of monks. Perhaps he is referring to pre-teenagers.

March 19
July 19
November 18

40. On the Measure of Drink

1 Cor. 7:7

[1]"Everyone has his special gift from God, one this and another that"; [2]and so it is with some hesitation that we lay down how much others should eat or drink. [3]Nevertheless, taking into consideration the needs of the less strong, we believe that half a measure of wine a day is enough for each; [4]but those to whom

God gives the ability to abstain should know that they will have a special reward.

[5]If local conditions, work or the summer heat call for a greater amount, let it be at the superior's discretion; but he must always be very careful that intemperance and drunkenness do not creep in.

[6]We read that wine is definitely not for monks, yet because it is impossible to persuade monks of that nowadays, let us at least agree on this, to drink sparingly and not to the point of intemperance, [7]for

Sir. 19:2   "wine makes even the wise fall away."

[8]However, when local conditions determine that the aforesaid measure cannot be had, but much less or even none at all, those who live there must bless God and not grumble. [9]Above all do we urge that there should be no grumbling.

In our day many superfluities have become "necessities". This chapter has a wider application than it did when it was written. Wine was a bit of a luxury; after all, water was available. But monks, some of them, had come from a wine-producing countryside, and these could not be persuaded to change their habit of drinking it. So St Benedict – who one suspects was somewhat severe on wine-bibbing – gives way, simply on the grounds that these people cannot be persuaded to give it up. After all wine is a gift of God. But immediately he praises the ones who can do without.

We can apply this chapter in so many areas – smoking, snuff, a sundowner, silk shirts, taxis compared with public transport . . .

Wine has given place to spirits for some. For many moderation spells disaster; for these the only solution is total abstention, with

an honest admission that we are alcoholics: that is, one drink of alcohol leads on to drunkenness as dusk leads to darkness. We kid ourselves that while others are weak, we are strong.

We cannot free ourselves from so many addictions: gambling, sweets, fine clothes, "watching the box", trashy novels. All these and an endless catalogue of others have two effects: the first is that they become our idols, our be-all and end-all, and secondly that everything and everyone, God included, gives way before them. No time to read the Bible, to pray, to go to Mass! Really, we mean: no inclination. All our holy desires have been sucked away by our particular addiction. The second effect is waste of wealth, our money which could have been used in a multitude of ways serviceable to others and ourselves.

The final sentences of the chapter are also important for all of us. Suppose we do not have the funds to buy the many luxuries, to which we have been accustomed, then let us "bless God". Why bless God? Because this will wean us from soft living, keep us humble, give us a chance to share in the poverty of Christ, not only the Christ of long ago, but the Christs in their millions all round us.

41. The Times for the Brethren's Meals

March 20
July 20
November 19

[1]From holy Easter until Pentecost, the brethren should have dinner at the sixth hour and supper in the evening. [2]From Pentecost throughout the summer, unless the monks have work in the fields or the summer heat is oppressive, they should fast until the ninth hour on Wednesday and Friday. [3]On other days they should have dinner at the sixth hour. [4]If they have work in the fields or the summer heat is very intense, they

should go on having dinner at the sixth hour, as the abbot decides; [5]for he should so adjust and arrange everything that souls may be saved and the brethren do their work without justifiable grumbling.

[6]From the 13th September until the beginning of Lent, they should always have their meal at the ninth hour. [7]In Lent itself, until Easter, they should eat in the evening. [8]Vespers, however, should be so timed that they have no need of lamplight as they eat, but everything may be finished by daylight. [9]Indeed, at all times, the hour of supper or the evening meal should be so arranged that everything can be done by daylight.

The times of meals do not concern us acutely; they vary with countries and climates, customs and cultures. St Benedict is, however, here regulating for the various times of fasting, the Church's fasting periods and the monastic. In modern times the Church lays less stress on physical fasts and so too do monks. But it would be a real spiritual loss if the principle and practice of asceticism in food were thought to be obsolete, even if modern spiritual writers and saints in the tradition of St Francis of Sales point out the almost infinite variety of possible occasions now available to all for practising self-denial, without concentrating on asceticism with food. St Benedict himself seems more interested in the asceticism of the tongue. It would be tedious to enumerate each time he strikes out at murmuring; actual silence too is a favourite with him. Nevertheless we are many of us greedy, if not in the quantity consumed, then in delicacies sought.

First then we should desire to be simple in our tastes and then moderate in our eating and drinking.

Note that this once in the Rule St Benedict says that the brethren may have a just cause for grumbling, and the abbot should avoid giving them such a cause. Does this mean they should grumble? No, but if they do then it will be the superior on whom most of the blame will fall.

42. That No One Should Speak after Compline

March 21
July 21
November 20

[1]Monks should be zealous about silence at all times, but especially at night. [2]Consequently, whether fast day or non-fast day, this should always be the practice. [3]On days when there is a second meal, as soon as they have risen from supper, they should all sit together and one of them read the "Conferences" or "Lives of the Fathers", or at any rate, something that will edify the listeners; [4]but not the Heptateuch or Kings, because it will not be helpful for the weak-minded to hear these scriptures at that hour. They should be read at other times. [5]On fast days, there should be a short space between Vespers and the reading of the "Conferences", as we have said.

[6]As regards the reading, four or five pages should be read, or as many as time permits. [7]This reading period will allow everyone to gather together, whatever special task any may be engaged on.

[8]Then, when they are all assembled in the same place, they should say Compline; and on leaving Compline, there

should be no permission for anyone to speak further. [9]If anyone is found to transgress this rule of silence, he should be subjected to severe punishment; [10]except on occasions when guests make it necessary or the abbot happens to give someone an order. [11]Even then, the manner of speaking should be very serious and properly restrained.

No one can fail to notice that the Rule is determined to establish silence and never more than at night after the last public prayer, Compline. Curiously St Benedict does not say why, nor was he very explicit in the chapter on silence itself. A reason for this emphasis on night-time silence might simply be to ensure that all can get to sleep and not be disturbed. It would be particularly important in a group of twenty or more, all of whom went to bed in the same room and had to rise very early indeed to pray at dawn.

In St Benedict's monastery the monks would get their seven hours sleep as they went to bed at nightfall, while in the winter months, eight hours and more. But modern western-style man, with the aid of artificial light can easily reduce the hours of sleep according as he wishes. Night has become day.

In the mind of St Benedict silence had a deeper significance: the opportunity to listen to God in prayer, a truth so evident to the early monks that he takes it as said and never mentions it.

In our time the opposite is true: noise and talk, newspapers, radio and television, sounds of planes and cars and trucks are so pervasive at all times, night and day, that one points out how extraordinary in the history of the earth this is. Silence is a luxury, or more likely, for some, a threat like a gaping fathomless hole in the earth. We are frightened of it, turn on the "box", escape from ourselves, pour out a stiff drink. But we are not alone. "Come to me all you who labour and who are heavily burdened and I will give you rest" (Matt. 11:28).

This chapter also goes into the matter of good reading, proposing that just before Compline, last thing at night, the community should gather together to read a passage from the Bible or the Conferences (of Cassian) or lives of the Fathers (of the Desert). St Benedict is aware of the danger of reading anything which could too easily arouse the imagination and the passions in the night. This applies to anyone. But the important point is his encouragement of good reading. The Bible first, then the lives of the saints. We have been surfeited with over-pious versions of the latter. Matter-of-fact ones do exist, which concentrate on the development of their holiness from being just like us; on their virtues and good works, less on the miracles.

43. *On Those who Come Late to the Work of God or to Table*

March 22
July 22
November 21

[1]As soon as the signal for an hour of the divine office is heard, they should lay aside whatever they have in hand and assemble as quickly as possible, [2]yet in a dignified manner, without giving occasion to clownish behaviour. [3]Nothing, indeed, should be put before the Work of God.

[4]If anyone arrives at Vigils after the "Glory be to the Father" of Psalm 94, which we wish, therefore, to be said quite slowly and deliberately, he should not stand in his ordinary place in choir [5]but take the last place of all, or the one set apart by the abbot for such careless persons, that they may be seen by him and by all, [6]until at the end of the Work of God he does penance by public satisfaction. [7]Now, the reason for our

deciding that they ought to stand in the last place, or a place apart, is that, being seen by everyone, they will actually be shamed into amending. [8]For were they to remain outside the oratory, perhaps one would go back to bed and sleep, or doubtless sit down outside and give himself up to idle chatter, thereby giving an opportunity to the Evil One. [9]They should come inside instead, so that they do not lose the whole office and may amend for the future.

cf Eph. 4:27;
1 Tim. 5:14

[10]At the day hours, anyone who does not arrive at the Work of God until after the opening versicle and "Glory be to the Father" of the first psalm following must stand in the last place, in accordance with the ruling given above. [11]He must not presume to join the choir of those praying the psalms until he has made satisfaction, unless the abbot happens to pardon him and give permission. [12]Even so, the one at fault must still make satisfaction.

March 23
July 23
November 22

[13]Moreover, should anyone not come to table before the verse, so that all may say the verse and sit down at table together, [14]and should it be through his own carelessness or fault that he fails to arrive, he should be corrected up to twice. [15]If he still does not amend, he should not be allowed to share the common table, [16]but take his meals alone, apart from the company of everyone else, and be deprived of his allowance of wine until he has made satisfaction and amended. [17]Anyone not

present for the verse said after the meal should receive the same treatment.

[18]No one may presume to take any food or drink before or after the appointed hour; [19]but should anyone be offered something by a superior and refuse it, then, when he wants what he previously refused or something else, he is to receive nothing at all until he has made proper amends.

The lesson of this chapter is this. When the time has come for doing something we must immediately do it, whether it is setting off for our afternoon fresh-air exercise, getting out of bed when we intend, starting our studies on time, answering a bell or a telephone, or stopping some enthralling occupation for another more urgent though less attractive. Many an old monk would stop in the middle of transcribing a word, or before completing a sentence if the bell for the Divine Office rang. These are little unspectacular opportunities for self-control and for doing God's will, fitting in with his design.

St Benedict wants the monks to go to the choir "as quickly as possible", perhaps with the "deliberate speed" of the Hound of Heaven, because he adds, "nothing, indeed, should be put before the work of God" (v.3). In this spirit the monks go to their task, "in a dignified manner", gravely, recollectedly, seriously. Monks tearing about to arrive on time indicates a lack of peace.

There follow various graded penalties for those who arrive late for the Divine Office or meals. St Benedict has a down-to-earth idea of how easily a penance can turn into an occasion of further failure. Leave the lazy monks, who have not risen for Matins, outside the oratory, and all they will do is either crawl back to bed or squat at the door and gossip. No, they must come into choir.

44. On How the Excommunicated Are to Make Satisfaction

March 24
July 24
November 23

[1]Anyone excommunicated for serious faults from both the oratory and the table should prostrate himself, without a word, at the door of the oratory as the Work of God is coming to an end. [2]He should simply lie with his face to the ground, at the feet of all as they leave the oratory; [3]and should go on doing so until the abbot judges that he has made satisfaction. [4]Then, at the abbot's bidding, he should prostrate himself at the feet of the abbot and afterwards at the feet of everyone else, that they may pray for him; [5]only then, if the abbot so orders, should he be readmitted to the choir, in the rank the abbot appoints. [6]All the same, he must not presume to intone a psalm or lesson or anything else in the oratory unless the abbot grants further permission. [7]Moreover, at every hour, as the Work of God is reaching its close, he must prostrate himself on the ground in the place where he is standing, [8]and must continue to make satisfaction in this way until the abbot again tells him to stop.

[9]Those excommunicated for less serious faults from the table only, however, should make satisfaction in the oratory for as long as the abbot orders. [10]They must go on doing so until he blesses them and says, "That is enough."

The Rule does not expressly state what the serious faults are which deserve the excommunications from the Work of God in choir and from the common table. It is precise as to the manner of doing penance: (i) a mute prostration; (ii) a kneeling before the Abbot and each of his brethren, begging pardon; (iii) re-admission to choir and the refectory, but with no official duty; (iv) a final forgiveness by the Abbot.

This problem of restoring peace after a quarrel, or failure by one of the monks in a human relationship, is difficult to solve. It requires virtue on both sides of the quarrel or failure, not only true humility but magnanimity, a sense of love on the part of the offended party.

The longer it is left unresolved the more it festers, becoming an open sore until amputation may appear to be the only way out. Simply to say "I am sorry", but not mean it, provides no answer, because the other person knows by instinct this little speech is not genuine. On the other hand what rankles in the heart of the "offender" may be that the "offended" was as much responsible for the break as he was himself.

These situations demand great honesty in assessing one's own responsibility. If we are cause of the quarrel to any extent, we must be truthful and acknowledge it. Then the other, seeing true sorrow, will feel drawn to do the same.

What St Benedict is doing – in line with the tradition of the very early Church – is to ensure that the one who has done the wrong to the community, openly admits it with sorrow and humility.

45. On Those Who Make Mistakes in the Oratory

March 25
July 25
November 24

[1]If anyone makes a mistake in the recitation of a psalm, responsory, antiphon or lesson and does not humble himself by making satisfaction before all, he should be subjected to more severe punishment, [2]because he would not make good by humility a fault committed through carelessness. [3]Children, however, should be smacked for such a fault.

St Benedict goes on harrying those who make mistakes, partly of course because mistakes in community acts tend to upset the peace of the community, but far more to stamp out pride in the one who has made the mistake. Proud people cannot admit they make mistakes. This is a tremendous obstacle to holiness. Without a recognition of our limitations, our failures, our fundamental inadequacy, there is no possibility of progress in the life of the spirit. This is the danger for those who aim at the end but not the means.

Perfectionists are those who are never satisfied with their own performance. Humility is always present if we accept our limitations.

There are some useful and apparently contradictory aphorisms which deserve pondering and discussing. "The best is the enemy of the good"; "If a thing is worth doing it is worth doing well", and someone added: "If a thing is worth doing, it is worth doing badly".

46. On Those Who Commit Faults in Any Other Matters

March 26
July 26
November 25

[1]If anyone commits a fault in the course of his work, whether in the kitchen, in the storeroom, while serving, in the bakehouse, in the garden, while at work

at any craft or in any place, [2]if he breaks or loses anything, or is at fault in any other way, [3]and does not immediately, of his own accord, come before the abbot and community to confess his fault [4]but it becomes known through someone else, he must undergo more severe correction.

[5]If, however, the source of offence is concealed in his conscience, he should disclose it only to the abbot or to his spiritual elders, [6]who know how to heal both their own wounds and the wounds of others without revealing them and making them public.

Once again the Rule is determined to corner those who from pride cannot admit they have done something wrong, whether by breaking something or losing something. If they fail to recognize their faults, this, in itself perhaps minor, now becomes a failure of humility as well as a deception. This needs correcting.

This chapter breaks new ground in suggesting that we should seek spiritual help, spiritual healing. True, this idea already occurs in passing in chapter 4 and of course it is strong in the stream of monastic tradition – both Anthony and Pachomius put themselves under another hermit when they began, as too did Benedict himself. We all need to have a check upon our own ideas as these are so easily influenced by desires. A sacrament is waiting to be used, that of Reconciliation, or Confession, where we are cleansed from our sins by Christ's death and resurrection. We meet him through his minister; he comes to us in compassion and understanding and we can have confidence that our sins have been forgiven. This meeting is a great moment of grace, a healing opportunity and an encouragement in our weakness.

We need then to seek advice from another. These are old sayings: "A stitch in time saves nine", and "Two heads are better than one", and "Ask advice and you will not regret it". Out with it and what seemed a mountain will prove to be a molehill.

47. On Indicating the Hour for the Work of God

March 27
July 27
November 26

[1]To make known, day and night, the hour for the Work of God is to be the abbot's responsibility. He must either do so himself, or entrust this duty to a conscientious brother, so that everything may be done at the proper time.

[2]Psalms and antiphons are to be intoned by those appointed to do so, after the abbot according to rank. [3]But no one should presume to sing or read unless he can perform this service to the edification of the listeners; [4]for it must be done with humility, dignity and reverence, and by one whom the abbot has authorized.

In these chapters of the Rule, dealing with punishments, discipline, excommunications and the like, it is not these that are important for us but the failures and faults which call them forth. The forms of discipline or punishment, the sanctions or restraints, vary from age to age and country to country, but the "unsocial actions" remain pretty much the same. Therefore what a commentator should do is pinpoint what St Bendict is objecting to and see how these failures occur in our own lives. This will help the smooth running of a household, of a community.

When a group has to do anything together, the first thing needed is orderliness, and so St Benedict makes the abbot himself responsible for giving the signal for the work to begin, or if not him then he selects a careful brother who will be charged with the matter. Intoning of psalms or antiphons can be a cause of distraction to the brethren, therefore let it be done not with pride or pomp but humility, not in a slipshod or slapdash way, but gravely, and remembering always before whom we sing and therefore do so with reverence and awe. No one should be appointed who would cause distraction by his inadequacy.

These thoughts and suggestions apply to lay people who now frequently share in the ministry of the liturgy: as readers, giving holy communion, preparing the young for the sacraments; they apply in one's own prayers, which get hurried, thoughtless, careless – that morning or evening prayer, not infrequently pushed by the daily chores into the corner. Better to say a little slowly within the time now available than to scamper through it all, without any attention except to the clock.

48. On Daily Manual Labour

March 28
July 28
November 27

[1]Idleness is the enemy of the soul. Therefore, at given times the brethren ought to be occupied in manual labour, and again at other times in prayerful reading. [2]Accordingly, we believe that the times for each may be established as follows.

[3]From Easter until the 1st October, the morning – from after Prime until about the fourth hour – should be spent doing whatever work has to be done. [4]From the fourth hour until Sext, they should devote themselves to reading. [5]But after Sext, when they have risen from table, they may rest on their beds in complete silence; or anyone who wants to read by himself may do so, but without disturbing the others. [6]None should be said slightly early, half-way through the eighth hour; then again they should do whatever work needs to be done until Vespers. [7]Should local conditions or their poverty make it necessary for them to do

the harvesting themselves, they must not be disgruntled; [8]because then they are genuinely monks, when they live by the work of their hands, like our fathers and the apostles. [9]Yet everything should be done with moderation, on account of the faint-hearted.

March 29
July 29
November 28

[10]From the 1st October until the beginning of Lent, they should devote themselves to reading until the end of the second hour. [11]Terce should then be said; thereafter until None, all should work at the jobs assigned them. [12]At the first signal for the hour of None, all should lay aside their work in order to be ready for the second signal. [13]Then, after the meal, they should devote themselves to their reading or to the psalms.

[14]During the days of Lent, they should devote themselves to reading from the morning until the end of the third hour; and from then until the tenth hour they should do the work assigned to them. [15]In these days of Lent they should each receive a book from the library, to be read straight through in its entirety. [16]These books are to be given out at the beginning of Lent. [17]It is most important, however, that one or two seniors should be deputed to go round the monastery at the times when the brethren are free for reading, [18]to see that no brother is so wanting in fervour that he wastes his time in idleness and chatter, thereby not only doing himself no good but also proving a hindrance to others. [19]Should anyone like that be found – God forbid – he should be reproved a first and second

time. [20]If he fails to amend, he must be subjected to the punishment of the Rule, as a warning to the rest. [21]Moreover, brother ought not to associate with brother at inappropriate times.

March 30
July 30
November 29

[22]On Sunday, likewise, all should give themselves up to reading, except those assigned to various duties. [23]If anyone is so lacking in zeal and wanting in application that he either will not or cannot study or read, he must be given some work to do so that he may not be idle.

[24]Sick or less strong brethren should be given some kind of work or occupation to prevent them from being idle or, on the other hand, worn down by excessive toil and driven to flight. [25]The abbot must take their lack of strength into account.

It is not the precise hours of work and reading that matter so much as the first principle laid down in the first words of the chapter: idleness is the enemy of the soul. It is for this reason that throughout the Rule the whole day is regulated, if flexibly. My suspicion is that this meticulous care comes from St Benedict's years as a hermit. A solitary has to live by a fixed programme. Christians imprisoned and in solitary confinement for their faith for years on end, in countries behind the Iron Curtain, have repeatedly said that to avoid mental breakdown every hour of the day had to have its appointed task.

In the world the situation can often be the opposite with so much to do and with too little time to do it in. This is true of many: mothers of families, business people, workers in factories, in hospitals. But for the retired, the widowed, the unemployed, the words of the Rule still apply. Have a plan for the day, the week; stick to it, with flexibility.

St Benedict divides his day into three major occupations –

besides meals and a siesta – manual work, spiritual reading and prayer in choir. Today manual labour is least esteemed, lowest paid. So it was in his time. Slaves were forced to it. But he raised it to a godly occupation as Christ had done. When we have to labour with our hands, St Benedict writes, we should be happy to share in the workers' lot. Jesus was a worker.

Whatever is done – if not of itself immoral – for a livelihood is ennobled by that very fact, since it is sharing in the activity of God in his creative, sustaining work. Creation is not a static thing, a once-and-for-all. It progresses and develops; we human beings are among the chief agents of this continued development. First there is our own human growth, physical, mental and spiritual, all of which require appropriate work by parents, teachers, farmers for our food, cloth-makers, builders of houses, merchants and so on. Then there are agents of exchange, buying and selling. Next, the need for transport, the inventors, engineers, electricians, scientists, medical people; those who defend us, those who care for the common good, the entertainers; those who help us to relax, the newsagents, the thinkers, writers, artists. The Spirit needs priests and prophets, healers in the Church. If we perform our part in producing a civilized common life, in justice, truth and love, then we are co-operating in God's continuing creative work, that in all things, all actions, God may be glorified.

So the monk working away at his allotted task, the housewife and the worker at theirs, all share with God in his divine plan, and should praise the Lord.

This energetic chapter has, however, two gentle admonitions: the first to encourage a siesta and let no one disturb those having their snooze; the second is more general: let all be done with moderation so as not to distress the fainthearted, the weak.

Although the chapter heading proclaims that it is concerned with manual work, in fact it also treats of spiritual reading or lectio divina.

The reason for this intrusion of spiritual reading at this point seems to be that he wishes to complete the use of time still available after allocating the necessary hours to the divine office, to meals and to manual work, as well as keeping an eye on the *shifting amount of time available between sunrise and sunset through the year.*

The amount of time available seems to be three hours, more or less. It would include the study of scripture and learning the short passages, each day, by heart. It might even include learning to read – How many in St Benedict's time knew how to read? – but primarily that time is given to prayerful, meditative reading.

The Rule itself presumes monks' reading is mainly that of holy scripture, the word of God, but does mention St Basil the Great (c. 330–379), one of the founders of monastic life in the Eastern Church, also the writings of Cassian (360–435). Today we have huge numbers of books churned out by that amazing example of human ingenuity, the modern printing press. St Benedict might have been appalled. His idea of reading, and that of his predecessors was to do it in company with MEDITATION which meant learning by heart those parts that had struck home. These parts learnt by heart were, so to say, garnered in the storehouse of the memory to provide the food for the spirit during the rest of the day.

Obviously this practice with the Bible is supremely rewarding, but likewise it could be applied to much of St Benedict's Rule and the Imitation of Christ. *It is easy to see that both the Rule and the* Imitation *are writings of people who had done precisely that themselves, being penetrated with remembered passages, sentences, phrases from scripture and the Fathers. So, spiritual reading is not reading much, but pondering and remembering deeply.*

Is that possible outside in the modern world? Yes, not only possible or probable, but certain. It can be done by having one's own special precious slim small book which contains a very rich spiritual diet; this could be kept either at the bedside, in the pocket or in the purse. It could be a New Testament, *an* Imitation, *a* Rule of St Benedict, *a* Prayer of the Church, *for in this book – whichever it is – are stored brilliant stones or gems of divine wisdom. Gaze at one, fresh each morning and evening, or for each new day, or week . . .*

This chapter also describes how all monks should receive a book – possibly a manuscript of one of the books of the Bible – at the beginning of Lent. Then they could read their chosen book straight through from the beginning to the end. We are, some of us, tempted to flit from book to book, like butterflies that flop and balance over lots of blooms, never sitting. We leave out perhaps the preface, skip the introduction, skim over paragraphs, jump to the chapter with the interesting title, become disappointed, put down the book, start another. St Benedict finds that unsatisfactory, like travelling a big country by air, or along the super-highway: you never get deep into the countryside, the feel of it.

Real reading is a form of absorption. The book has to be worth that. If someone is engrossed in reading, let him be. Some monks, and others too, may be burdened with other work. Let them be excused much reading. Some may be going through a time of dryness, let them be excused; but St Benedict would encourage them to do something useful instead. Those who suffer from illness likewise should not feel guilty at failure to recite many psalms or do much reading. Their suffering is their prayer, just saying "Yes, Lord". All this is applicable to all of us.

49. On the Observance of Lent

March 31
July 31
November 30

[1]The life of a monk ought always to have a Lenten quality; [2]but since few are capable of that, we therefore urge the whole community during these days of Lent to lead lives of surpassing purity, [3]and in this holy season wash away the negligences of other times. [4]That may be properly done by abstaining from all sinful habits and devoting ourselves to prayer with tears, to reading, to compunction of heart and self-denial. [5]During these days, therefore, let us add something to the usual measure of our service, such as private prayers and

cf 1 Thess. 1:6

abstinence from food and drink, [6]that each one, of his own free will and with the joy of the Holy Spirit, may offer God something over and above the measure appointed for him. [7]That is to say, let him deny himself some food, drink, sleep, pointless conversation and banter, and look forward to holy Easter with joy and spiritual longing.

[8]Each one, however, must tell his abbot what he is offering up, for it must be done with his blessing and approval. [9]Whatever is done without the spiritual father's permission is to be attributed to presumption and vainglory, unworthy of reward. [10]Everything, therefore, must be done with the abbot's approval.

Change "monk" to "Christian" in paragraph one and the suggestions remain true. Christians are not of this world. But being in it, we cannot help being contaminated. That does not mean that a Christian has to be dour or grim, far from it. We should, as Christians, find ourselves free and happy. But to disentangle ourselves from the frivolities and luxuries of the material life is difficult. So St Benedict says, "Let us add something to the usual measure" during Lent. He makes a few suggestions.

Be pure in heart: by which he means single-minded in our desire to serve God. We have neglected our good habits, perhaps, in prayer, at talk, in eating, in drinking. He goes on: be rid of all vices; pray with sorrow for our sins – even to tears; take up good reading, practise abstinence, that is restraint in eating and drinking. St Benedict wants this all done voluntarily, meaning over and above the normal. This is the only place where he encourages this personal, almost individualistic approach, to the spiritual life. Usually he is saying: let everything be done as the

Rule lays down. Of course, even that is voluntary, requiring a personal assent. One could at any time "walk out", not that to do such a thing would be right. But a good practice can be mere habit, and he is reminding us to do good in a willing way. For lay people, Lent is not so much taking on new devotions or new penances, as realizing that what is done could be done for a better motive than routine, since everything can be God's work. This is what God wants me to do NOW. Love my neighbours, work with integrity for love of them, because this is part of God's plan; help others for love of Christ who himself loved them. What prayers we do say, we will go on saying, not because we once, perhaps long ago, determined to keep them up – a good motive – but because to pray is to keep in direct touch with our creator, our Saviour, our life, because praying is making us alive to those divine truths which will one day fill our whole horizon.

Ages ago, we gave up sugar or salt in food or drink; now we prefer it so. The idea had been restraint, control of desire by our will. Now it is habit – a good one. Why not use that money, saved, to help those who do not even have the food or drink in which to put that sugar or salt? We are often sad at the famine in the world. Here is a positive way to help.

We have realized that it is possible to be more considerate in the home. No amount of self-denial is of use unless we show genuine concern for others, which is true love. We used to get to Mass on a weekday. That could be revived.

A most helpful practice is to discuss with a wise person, priest or lay person, what we should do about Lent each year. To discuss is like dusting and spring cleaning. This discloses the "dusty" corners of our lives. For lay people this could be the equivalent of the final sentence of this chapter, "Everything, therefore, must be done with the abbot's approval".

50. On Brethren Working at a Distance from the Oratory or on a Journey

April 1
August 1
December 1

[1]Brethren who are working a long way away and are unable to return to the oratory at the proper time, [2]and are recognized by the abbot to be in such a position, [3]should perform the Work of God in their workplace, kneeling out of reverence for God.

[4]Similarly, those sent on a journey should not omit the appointed hours but say them by themselves as best they can, and not neglect to perform their measure of service.

This chapter brings up two cases of monks away from their normal round of prayer with the community. What should they do? The answer given: to say your prayers where you are and make some outward signs of reverence. It is a common experience: change the setting and the habitual pious practices slip away. We always say "Oh! when things settle down, I'll get back to saying my prayers, take up reading, daily Mass. No, not today, but tomorrow". The Spanish for tomorrow is mañana" and has almost the meaning of "never". The sign of the cross, kneeling, finding a church: these steady us in change.

51. On Brethren Who Do Not Go Far Distant

April 2
August 2
December 2

[1]A brother sent on some kind of business and expected to return to the monastery the same day should not presume to eat outside, even if strongly urged to do so, [2]unless the abbot happens to have authorized him. [3]If he acts otherwise, he should be excommunicated.

Going out of the monastery just for the day for whatever purpose, business, visiting the sick, a dentist, a lecture, saying Mass – there are a hundred and one good reasons – must be under permission from the abbot. It is the "aside" incidents that the Rule is concerned about. We may have one open purpose, another hidden one may lurk in the background. This is true of all of us. We should be honest with our abbot – if we are monks – and also with our consciences, whether we are monks or not. Truthfulness, honesty with ourselves and with others will save us from many a possible fatal attraction. A meal is a time of intimacy: that is why St Benedict puts his finger there, and wants to know where his monks are being entertained. The Rule is a kind of assistance to conscience.

52. On the Oratory of the Monastery

April 3
August 3
December 3

[1]The oratory should be what it is called, and nothing else should be done or kept there. [2]At the end of the Work of God, all should go out in perfect silence, with reverence for God, [3]so that any brother who may wish to pray by himself will not be prevented by someone else's bad behaviour. [4]Furthermore, if at other times someone wishes to pray privately, he should simply go in and pray, not in a loud voice, but with tears and devotion of heart. [5]Anyone, therefore, who does not act like that is not to be allowed to remain in the oratory once the Work of God is over, in case he proves a hindrance to someone else.

So often an oratory, even the parish church, is not available. To find a place to pray by oneself privately seems impossible. But today lay people have to follow St Francis of Sale's advice and seek the most inward corner of our being. It has to be kept clear and clean of all clutter and stain which passes through the mind, unwanted, and not least from the newspapers or the "box". There, to that secret place, we can withdraw. So "simply go and pray".

We have to find little or larger stretches of time, before the evening meal or after breakfast, away from the telephone, away from all interruptions, and we can say, "God I trust you". "Not in a loud voice", but "with tears and devotion", not of the voice, but "of the heart", unseen, unheard, except by God.

Over-pious demonstrations can soon "prove a hindrance to someone else" particularly a husband or wife whose religion perhaps is not exuberant in that way.

53. *On the Reception of Guests*

April 4
August 4
December 4

Matt. 25:35

Gal. 6:10

[1]All guests who come should be welcomed like Christ, for he himself will say, "I was a stranger and you made me welcome." [2]Appropriate honour should be shown to all, but especially to "members of the household of faith" and to pilgrims. [3]Accordingly, once a guest has been announced, the superior and brethren should go and meet him with a truly loving courtesy. [4]First of all, they should pray together and so be united in peace; [5]but the kiss of peace must not be exchanged unless prayer has preceded it because of the delusions of the devil. [6]In greeting all guests, on arrival or as they depart, great humility should be shown. [7]By a bow of the head or the complete prostration of the body on the ground, Christ is to be worshipped; for he is indeed received in them.

[8]After the guests have been welcomed, they should be invited to pray; then the superior or someone appointed by him should sit with them. [9]The Law of God should be read in the guest's presence, for his edification; and then every kindness should be shown him. [10]The superior may break his fast for the sake of a guest, unless it is a special fast day which may not be dispensed; [11]but the brethren should keep the customary fasts. [12]The abbot should offer the guests water for their hands; [13]both the abbot and the whole community should wash the feet of all the guests. [14]After they have

washed them, they should say this verse:

Ps. 47(48):10 "O God, we have experienced your mercy in the midst of your temple."

[15]Meticulous care and attention should be shown in welcoming poor people and pilgrims, because in them especially Christ is received. The awe which the rich inspire is obviously enough of itself to command them respect.

April 5
August 5
December 5

[16]The kitchen for the abbot and guests should be separate, so that when guests – who are never wanting in a monastery – arrive at unexpected times, the brethren may not be disturbed. [17]Two brethren capable of doing the work well should be assigned to this kitchen for the year. [18]Help should be given them when needed so that they may serve without grumbling. On the other hand, when they have less to do, they should go wherever other jobs are assigned to them. [19]Moreover, not only to them but in all the departments of the monastery, the same consideration should be shown [20]and help provided when needed. Conversely, whenever they are free they should do whatever is required.

[21]The guest-house should be entrusted to a brother who is God-fearing to the depths of his soul. [22]A proper supply of bedding should be kept there, and the house of God looked after by wise people in a wise way.

[23]No one without specific instructions is to associate or talk with guests; [24]but if he meets or catches sight of one, he should greet him humbly, as we said, and ask a blessing, then pass on,

explaining that he is not allowed to talk
with a guest.

*St Benedict is in two minds about guests. On the one hand he has
the words of Jesus ringing in his ears – and he begins with those –
"I was a stranger and you made me welcome" (Matt. 25:35); on
the other he is anxious to preserve his monks from contamination
from the world. So he swings from one side to the other; the
longing to do everything one would do when receiving Christ
himself, and trying to prevent disturbing the quiet, the peace, of
the monastery. The whole community should receive the guest,
wash his feet, or the abbot do it alone while the monks should cast
their eyes down and not speak a word.*

*In practice there are guest masters who with the abbot receive
all the guests. Individual monks help either when there is need or
when the guest has come to see that member of the community.*

*St Benedict also sets up an outer rampart, a kindly, peaceful,
discreet old monk who should be posted at the gate of the
monastery. You might say "tethered there". The Rule also speaks
of a special refectory kitchen, kitcheners and servers for the
guests. St Benedict desires to protect the quiet of the monks and
so he keeps his two views in tension; the reception of guests and
the silence of the monastery. He divides the guests into
categories: the rich, who know how to look after themselves –
human instinct serves them; and the poor in whom the monk
should see Christ more than in any others, and with these he
would put the pilgrims. There is also the distinction between the
members of God's household, that is the faithful and those outside
the Church. It is the former who, he says, should get special
treatment.*

*How does this concern the householder today? In the first place
it is good to form a bond with those of the faith, by friendship and
hospitality; it creates a true and strong Christian community. It
is prudent to bring up children in a faith-filled atmosphere. Nor
are adults immune from pagan, un-Christian talk and behaviour.
Not that we should live in a ghetto or have no contact with our*

neighbours, whether Protestant, Jewish, Muslim, Hindu or pagan. Nevertheless, we are weak in sensuality, in our ignorance, vanity, ambition.

A far-reaching good can be done by the helpful friendship of a strong Catholic family towards our sick neighbours, towards the lonely ones and the old. Isolated children and one-parent families: these need help.

What should we do about the professional beggar? Give food and drink, clothes, not normally money. Be very kind but firm. "Believe all things", but act very prudently.

St Benedict makes a special point about the faith of the guest. Today we are once again embedded in a non-believing or half-believing world. In our homes we should distinguish, receive all as Christ, yes, because he is there, but often in the "chains" of unbelief. We may think we are strong, yet, if all mention of faith, which we hold dear, has to be avoided – I am thinking of habitual guests – then things of the faith fall into the background, then become taboo in our subconscious mechanism of choice. We stunt our faith, and, given some great moral shock, one morning we will find our faith is dead. With real open friendship in which differences are eagerly discussed, such encounters can stimulate our faith.

54. Whether a Monk Should Receive Letters or Anything Else

April 6
August 6
December 6

[1]Under no circumstances shall a monk be allowed to receive letters, blessed tokens, or any little presents whatever, from his parents or other people or one of the community, nor may he give any, without the abbot's permission. [2]If anything is sent to him, even by his parents, he must not presume to accept it unless it has been shown to the abbot beforehand.

Eph. 4:27;
1 Tim. 5:14

[3]If the abbot permits its acceptance, it remains his prerogative to decide to whom it should be given; [4]and the brother to whom it happened to be sent must not take it amiss, "lest opportunity be given to the devil." [5]Anyone who presumes to act otherwise should be subjected to the discipline of the Rule.

Possessions can be a serious obstacle in our search for God. One way of being rid of the obstacle is to be rid of personal possessions. This is the old monastic way. In this chapter St Benedict is blocking the holes so that the fox of possessiveness does not sneak in. Receive nothing, give nothing, he writes, without permission of the abbot. Remember our very bodies are not our own. All is God's and on loan.

In the world the ways of preventing possessions from getting out of hand have to be different. We speak of the right use of wealth. But the underlying principles are the same. Everything we have, has been given as a gift from God. Job recognized this: "God gave, God has taken away". We must therefore use whatever we have according to how God would want, but sharing with those who have less, little or none. On the Last Day we will be judged by that, as we know from the gospel. There are many ways of doing this and just as many of evading the issue.

A sign that money has become a god, is arrogance and contempt for or irritation with the poor.

55. On the Clothing and Footwear of the Brethren

April 7
August 7
December 7

[1]The clothing given to the brethren should correspond to the nature and climate of the place where they live, [2]because more is needed in cold districts but less in warm ones. [3]It is the abbot's responsibility to take this into consideration. [4]But in average places, we believe that it will be enough for each monk to have a tunic, a cowl – [5]a thick woollen one for winter, a thin or worn one for summer – [6]and a scapular for work; also footwear, both shoes and sandals. [7]The monks must not complain about the colour or coarseness of all these things but make do with what can be obtained in the district where they live and can be bought cheaply. [8]However, the abbot must take trouble about the measurements of these garments in order that they may not be too short for the wearers but fit properly.

[9]Whenever new clothes are received, the old ones should be returned straightaway and kept in a wardrobe for the poor. [10]It is enough for a monk to have two tunics and two cowls, to allow for nightwear and for the washing of these articles; [11]anything more is superfluous and should be taken away. [12]Footwear also, or anything else that is old, should be returned when new articles are received.

[13]Those sent on a journey should collect underwear from the wardrobe.

On their return, it should be washed and handed back. [14]Their cowls and tunics also should be slightly better than the ones they usually wear. They should get them from the wardrobe before setting out and return them when they come back.

April 8
August 8
December 8

[15]For bedding, a mat, a blanket, a coverlet and a pillow should be adequate. [16]The beds should be inspected frequently by the abbot, in case private possessions should be discovered there. [17]If anyone is found to have anything not given by the abbot, he must be subjected to very severe punishment. [18]In order that this evil practice of private ownership may be rooted out in its entirety, all necessary items are to be supplied by the abbot: [19]that is, cowl, tunic, sandals, shoes, belt, knife, pen, needle, handkerchief, and writing tablets. Thus, every excuse of needing something will be taken away. [20]Yet the abbot must constantly keep in mind that text from the *Acts 4:35* Acts of the Apostles, "Distribution was made to each according to need." [21]In the same way, therefore, the abbot should take into account the weaknesses of the needy, not the ill-will of the envious; [22]yet in all his decisions he must bear in mind the retribution of God.

Monks and nuns wear "habits", that is a distinctive dress of unworldly appearance, not scruffy, but simple and clean. The scholars have gone to town on this subject, partly because it is a little obscure – words shift their meanings – partly because we are all interested in dress – in fact in dressing up. St Benedict was in favour of simplicity and uniformity: a cowl and a tunic. By cowl he seems to have meant a hood, with perhaps something attached to it, round the shoulders. This gradually got longer till it became a kind of cloak or what we now call a cowl, a voluminous outer robe used only in choir. So, he proposed a hood, and secondly, a tunic or smock that went down below the knees. When going on a journey the monk should receive a fresh hood and tunic and underclothing. St Benedict makes no mention of a belt, an oversight because it is listed later in verse 19.

I agree with St Francis of Sales: those in the world should dress nicely to be attractive to their husband and wife, and the young to be attractive to all, but not lasciviously. On the other hand he told the widowed Jeanne de Chantal to "lower the sign", that is take off her elegant hat, unless she was looking for another husband. She obeyed.

In one sense those who have stopped wearing religious habits have gained an advantage in that they now appear as "one of the boys", and after all the "cowl" does not make the monk. Yet the habit is a real sign, a check, a reminder both to the wearer and others of what you are and what you should be.

Clothes are bought or made and worn from vanity. But as banks have to look safe and sound, not extravagant, so businessmen have to dress so as to appear honourable, safe, men of substance.

In Africa some tribes have the custom that wives must be very comfortably large to show that their husbands feed them well. So clothes can be just make-believe; but for certain categories of people, clothes, besides covering our nakedness and keeping us warm, are among the most important signs men and women use to give a message, whatever it may be. Policemen, postmen, clergy, soldiers, artists, nurses, sisters, monks and nuns, all developed their clothes as signs of what they stood for. Clothes are profoundly symbolic and not to be changed lightly. The veil, for instance, is a very old sign of virginity.

Why do we buy lots of clothes? Think on what we might do with the money if we did not. Also, what do we do with our old clothes? St Benedict advises his monks to give them to the poor.

Towards the end of the chapter is a list of the things that the monks normally have the use of: hood, tunic, sandals, shoes, belt,

*knife, pen, needle, handkerchief, writing tablets. This included
all that was needed by a monk for his personal use in those days.
Our novice master used to say that the practice of poverty was
seeing how much we could do without, like mountaineers who, in
order to reach the heights without being weighted down, "travel
light".*

*St Benedict, however, quotes from the Acts of the Apostles;
"Distribution was made to each according to need". He judged
these extra needs as weaknessess. Obviously they could be, but in
the modern times, the works that monks engage in, whether
manual or intellectual, are so varied and highly skilled, that the
"tools" of their trade are necessary and for their use: binding
tools, carpenter's tools, typewriters, computers, recorders.*

*So too in the world, all Christians need to follow Christ in his
poverty according as they are led by the Holy Spirit, not to be
extravagant but moderate in their use of what God has lent them,
to make sure they share what they possess with those who have
less, seeing that what they have in excess of their real needs
belongs truly to the needy. In our "village", the world, many are
starving.*

56. On the Abbot's Table

April 9
August 9
December 9

[1]The abbot's table should always be with guests and pilgrims. [2]However, when there are no guests, it shall be within his power to invite any of the brethren he wishes. [3]But, for the sake of maintaining discipline, one or two seniors should always be left with the brethren.

*St Benedict seems to expect the monastery always to have guests.
If occasionally there were none, he expected the abbot to invite
some monks to share meals with him. Conviviality is part of the
monastic spirit, but always with restraint and in moderation.*

57. On the Craftworkers of the Monastery

April 10
August 10
December 10

[1]If there are any craftworkers in the monastery, they should practise their crafts with complete humility, provided the abbot gives permission. [2]But if one of them becomes conceited because of his skill at his craft and imagines that he is conferring something on the monastery, [3]he should be taken away from his craft and not allowed to return to it unless, after he has humbled himself, the abbot again authorizes him to do so.

[4]If any of the craftworkers' work is to be sold, those responsible for the transaction must not have the presumption to practise any dishonesty. [5]Let them al-

cf Acts 5:1–11

ways remember Ananias and Saphira, [6]for fear that they and all who deal dishonestly with the monastery's goods should suffer spiritual death just as they incurred physical death. [7]As regards price, the evil of avarice must not sneak in. [8]Instead, goods should always be sold slightly more cheaply than is possible for

1 Pet. 4:11

people living in the world, [9]"that in all things God may be glorified."

Pride is the real danger for a monk who thinks he is good at something. A famous singer who, who when asked what were his thoughts on being brought back repeatedly before a wildly enthusiastic audience, replied, "Not to us, Lord, not to us, but to your name be the glory".

The last line of the chapter has become something of a Benedictine motto, "that in all things God may be glorified".

Monks do glorify God in choir; this is the Work of God par excellence, but here we have a clear statement: that we praise God in all things, too. Even in seemingly worldly matters God can and should be glorified: in the work of craftspersons, for example.

St Benedict is also anxious about the evil of avarice creeping in. We might add that undercutting too, can cause unfair hurt to others. In everything we do, it should be done justly and considerately and so give God glory.

St Benedict for the best of motives suggests undercutting competitors who sell produce that the monks are also marketing. This would not appeal to business people today, even good Christian business people. But the concluding sentence which provides St Benedict's motive is important. It runs as follows: "that in all things God may be glorified". This quotation from 1 Peter 4: 11 puts all things under the care of God, puts everything whatever – including prices of commodities – under God's scrutiny and care. We must not exclude any human thing from divine wisdom. We should do and endure all for God's glory. Our prayer, yes. But why not specially our every day lives? This is one of the insights of our time on lay spirituality, on how lay people can and should be serving, loving, praising God. The question is when should they be doing this; the answer is simple: at all times and in all things. So that everything in the whole universe may be returned to God as part of his one wise plan.

58. On the Procedure for Admitting Brethren

April 11
August 11
December 11

John 4:1

[1]A newcomer to monastic life should not be granted an easy entrance, [2]but as the apostle says, "Test the spirits, to see whether they come from God." [3]Therefore, if someone comes and keeps knocking, and if after four or five days he can be seen to be patiently putting up with his harsh treatment and the difficulty of gaining admission and is persistent in his request, [4]he should be allowed to enter and stay in the guest-house for a few days. [5]After that, he should stay in the novitiate, where the novices receive their formation, eat and sleep. [6]A senior with a talent for winning souls should be appointed to look after them with minute care. [7]His concern must be whether the novice is really seeking God, whether he has a zeal for the Work of God, for obedience and for things that humble him. [8]Let him be told frankly of all the difficulties and hardships through which we make our way to God.

[9]If he promises to persevere in his stability, at the end of two months this Rule should be read straight through to him, [10]and he should be told, "Look, this is the law under which you wish to serve. If you can observe it, enter; if you cannot, you are free to leave." [11]If he still stands his ground, he should then be taken back to the novitiate mentioned earlier, and again tested in all patience. [12]After six months have passed, the Rule

should be read to him in order that he may know on what he is embarking; [13]and if he still remains steadfast, after four months the Rule should be read to him again. [14]And if, after due consideration, he promises to observe everything and obey all the commands given him, let him be admitted to the community. [15]But he must realize that, according to the law of the Rule, from that day onwards he is no longer free to leave the monastery, [16]nor to withdraw his neck from the yoke of the Rule which, during so long a period of reflection, he was at liberty either to refuse or to accept.

April 12
August 12
December 12

[17]He is to be admitted in this way. In the oratory, in the presence of all, he is to promise stability, fidelity to the monastic way of life, and obedience; [18]and do so before God and his saints, that if he should ever act otherwise, he may be sure that he will be condemned by the one he mocks. [19]He must express his promise in a petition drawn up in the names of the saints whose relics are there and of the abbot who is present. [20]He should write the petition with his own hand, or if he is illiterate, someone else should do so at his request, with the novice himself putting his mark to it and placing it on the altar with his own hand. [21]After he has laid it there, the novice himself should immediately intone this

Ps. 118(119):116 verse, "Receive me, Lord, according to your word, and I shall live; do not disappoint me in my hope." [22]The whole community is to repeat the verse three times, adding "Glory be to the Father."

²³Then the new brother is to prostrate himself at the feet of each person, to ask them to pray for him. From that day onwards he is to be counted as one of the community.

²⁴If he owns anything, he must either give it to the poor beforehand or make a formal donation of it to the monastery; he is to retain nothing at all for himself, ²⁵being perfectly aware that henceforth he will have no power even over his own body. ²⁶Straightaway, therefore, in the oratory, he is to be stripped of everything of his own that he is wearing and dressed in the monastery's clothing. ²⁷But the clothes taken from him must be put into a wardrobe for safe-keeping. ²⁸Then, should he ever agree to the devil's prompting and leave the monastery – which God forbid – he may be stripped of the monastery's clothing and sent away. ²⁹But that petition of his, which the abbot took from the altar, is not to be returned to him but kept in the monastery.

Not all go through a noviciate before setting out on their life's work. It would be an excellent practice if we did, say before we embarked on the legal profession, on being a soldier, a businessman, a farmer, before we engaged on marriage. At least we would then have given deep thought on how best to make our chosen life Christ-like. This chapter has something to say to all of us setting off on our life's journey.

The novice is treated roughly, kept at the door for days. So are the young aspirants to the profession of medicine – doctors or nurses – who receive a gruelling period of training. The profession only wants the best. The young should have this explained to them. This could be enlarged upon for any way of life. The Rule has the often-quoted phrase, the "dura et aspera", *the hard uneven path. In other words, the monastic way leads to God, but the way is savage, rocky, stormy, not physically so much as demanding a strong spirit. So, too, many professions, ways of life – not least marriage – demand moral stamina, courage, doggedness, determination, staying power.*

In the Rule the novice must be under a monk who "has a talent for winning souls". We might call him a guide, a philosopher, a friend. The new hand must be prepared to follow the lead of such a one, and in the world he himself has to choose such a one. This requires wisdom and prudence. But who at that age has such gifts? It is not the "holiest" who is necessarily the wisest. What we should be looking for is a just man who shows calm balanced judgment. St Teresa of Avila, who had suffered from uninformed confessors, or guides, wanted above all – with holiness – one learned in the things of the Spirit, who would understand these matters even if he had not experienced them himself – and together with that, humility.

The test that St Benedict expects the novice master to apply, to discover whether the novice is truly seeking God or simply "escaping" or romanticizing, is this: is he eager for the divine office, for obedience, for trials? And in the world are eager Christians wilful or humble – which? Do they respond to difficulties not only with determination and resourcefulness, but also with patience and acceptance? One or two other suggestions of this chapter can also be useful for lay people. The first is this, that the effort being made by the beginner should be regularly under the keen and sympathetic eye of the guide or novice-master. This has many advantages: it saves time and energy from going off at tangents, down dead-end paths; it keeps beginners' spirits up when the going is very hard; they learn more readily from their mistakes; it saves them from pride on the one hand and despair on the other.

Learning to live a truly Christian lay life is a gradual thing, a slow awakening. Therefore, like a novice, we should have periodical check-ups, by a formal retreat, a day of recollection, a week-end retreat and once in a while, perhaps, even a week's retreat. The form of this "retreat" may vary, now one way, now another. But we should remember that this exercise is a conscious endeavour to be alone with God, not a spiritual rat-race, endless discourses and conferences about the life of the spirit, but actually living it, being immersed in the silence of God.

As one might expect in a chapter concerned with formation, there is mention of the Benedictine "vows": stability, obedience and conversion of manners. Stability seems a strange thing to promise, yet monks in the time of Benedict vowed, and still do, to stay put in one place for life, to remain in the monastery of their choice under obedience to the abbot. This has three important elements: the vow is, for life, to one particular group of people and to one abbot and his successors. This clearly has much in common with marriage, as we have known it in the Christian world: marriage is for life, it is a commitment to one person and to the family that God gives, a tremendous sense of stability. Without this life-long stable element, both marriage and monastic life flounder. The intimacy of both requires a certain degree of withdrawnness. In marriage we surrender ourselves to each other in total love and trust, jealous of each other's affections. Even the God of the Old Testament is known as a "jealous" God. A crisis is not the end of this love, but a new and deeper beginning and even an opening into a wider appreciation. The romantic start, the growth in friendship, the loving, sometimes heroic care for each other into old age, are elements of stability that both married people and monks enjoy.

Another of the vows which a Benedictine monk takes is "conversion of manners" or as it is translated in this Rule, "fidelity to the monastic way of life". In the unmarried state, this fidelity also has its counterpart. Unmarried lay persons, either choosing this state or finding themselves in it and deciding to remain single for the sake of God and perhaps of God's poor, clearly understand the difficulty of persevering in a particular way of life. There is no intention in these pages to turn lay people into monks or nuns while still living in the world. The vow is a vow to seek God in that way of life to which he has brought you, with its ups and downs.

59. On the Offering of the Children of the Nobility and of the Poor

April 13
August 13
December 13

[1]If any member of the nobility should offer his child to God in the monastery, and the boy himself is still very young, his parents are to draw up the petition mentioned above; [2]then, at the presentation of the gifts, they are to wrap the document itself and the boy's hand in the altar cloth and so offer him.

[3]As regards their property, they must promise under oath in the same document that they will never personally, nor through an intermediary, nor in any way whatever, nor at any time, give him anything or let him have any opportunity to possess anything. [4]But, of course, if they do not want to do this yet wish to offer the monastery something by way of alms for their own good, [5]they should make a formal donation of the property they want to give the monastery. They may keep back the income for themselves, if they wish. [6]And so every loophole should be closed, leaving no expectations to the boy by which he could be led astray and ruined – which God forbid – as we have learned by experience can be so.

[7]Poorer people are to do the same; [8]but those who have nothing at all are simply to draw up the petition and offer their son, in the presence of witnesses, at the presentation of the gifts.

The custom described here of offering one's son for life at a tender age to a monastery is no longer considered responsible – if it ever was. The accompanying ceremony is, however, revealing, and shows what an oblate offering also should be.

(1) *The offering is proclaimed in a document signed by the person himself or herself (not of course, in the case of a child, when the signing has to be done as in this chapter by the parents).*

(2) *The document is offered "with the gifts", which presumably are the bread and the wine at the offertory of the Mass. Not all commentators would agree with this understanding of the "gifts": it could mean "the gifts of the parents to the monastery".*

(3) *The boy's hand and the document are wrapped in the altar cloth. Today we put the document of commitment under the corporal – the piece of linen placed at the centre of the altar, on which are to stand the chalice and the paten.*

(4) *The purpose of this is to emphasize that the act of oblation is a sacrificial one, sharing in the sacrifice of Christ of whom after all we are members, and in whose offering of himself we want to share.*

St Benedict by a right instinct puts the ceremony for the vows in the heart of the Mass, in the place of sacrifice. One becomes an oblate in a similar manner.

60. On Priests Who May Wish to Live in the Monastery

April 14
August 14
December 14

[1]If anyone in priest's orders asks to be admitted to the monastery, assent should not be given him too quickly. [2]However, if he stoutly persists in his request, he must appreciate that he will have to observe the full discipline of the Rule, [3]with no mitigation on his behalf.

Matt. 26:50   Let it be as scripture says, "Friend, why
have you come?" [4]Nevertheless, he
should be allowed to stand next to the
abbot, to give blessings and to celebrate
Mass, provided that the abbot authorizes
him. [5]Otherwise, he must not presume
to take anything on himself, knowing
that he is subject to the discipline of the
Rule and ought rather to give everyone
an example of humility.

[6]If there is any question of an appointment or some other business in the
monastery, [7]he should take the place that
corresponds to the date of his entry into
the monastery, and not that granted him
out of respect for his priesthood.

[8]In the same way, if any clerics wish to
join the monastery, they should be
ranked somewhere in the middle, [9]but
only if they also promise to keep the Rule
and observe stability.

*This chapter is on "order", that is, each monk having due rank in
the community. Order is one of the elements of living that St
Benedict recognizes as providing peace. He is concerned that
those longest in the community should be given seniority of
order. It is very odd, but it seems natural, that the older members
of a family should be given respect. In every traditional society
this is thought essential. In China age has for thousands of years
been seen as the most honoured time of life. In Africa, still, the
old are reverenced. Perhaps the reason for this is that they are
thought to have treasured the ancestral wisdom.*

*To move now to the natural family and the children, the middle
ones easily become hiddenly obsessed with the thought that they
are ignored either because the older get all the attention, or
because the new baby is now the centre of attraction. On the other
hand, the eldest, who has been the only pebble on the beach, can
likewise feel ignored when two or three more appear, each*

receiving a share of the available attention and affection. It is important, far more important than many realize, for each and every one to receive due consideration and love.

Likewise, just as a priest being received into the community must not demand special privileges, so the old, received into the home of the young, must be careful not to demand special consideration in everything, though the young should try to ease the sense of being strangers that the old may feel.

61. On the Way in Which Visiting Monks Are to Be Received

April 15
August 15
December 15

[1]If a visiting monk comes from a long distance and wishes to stay in the monastery as a guest, [2]provided that he is content with the customs of the place as he finds them, and does not worry the monastery with excessive demands, [3]but is simply content with what he finds, he should be received for as long a time as he wishes. [4]If in a reasonable, humble, charitable way he makes any criticisms or observations, the abbot should prudently weigh them, in case the Lord sent him for the very purpose. [5]Then if, later on, he wishes to fix his stability permanently, his wish should not be denied, especially as his character could be assessed during the time that he was a guest.

April 16
August 16
December 16

[6]But if during that time he has been found too demanding or full of faults, not only ought he not to be made a member of the community, [7]but he should be politely told to depart, in case

others should be corrupted by his deplor-
able behaviour. [8]If, however, he is not
the kind of person who deserves to be
sent away, he should not merely be
accepted as a member of the community
if he asks, [9]he should even be pressed to
stay, so that others may profit by his
example; [10]and because wherever we are
we serve under the same Lord and fight
for the same King. [11]Moreover, the abbot
may give such a person a slightly higher
place in community, if he regards him as
worthy of it. [12]Similarly, not only in the
case of a monk, but also anyone in the
priestly or clerical orders mentioned
above, the abbot may give them a higher
rank than that which corresponds to
their date of entry, if he sees that their
life merits it. [13]The abbot must be careful,
however, not to receive into the community a monk from another known
monastery without the consent of the
monk's abbot and a letter of recommen-
Tob. 4:16   dation, [14]since it is written, "Do not do to
another what you do not want done to
yourself."

*Monasteries have visiting monks – some edifying, some not. You
in your houses have visitors – likewise some edifying, some not.
What to do? Encourage those who are, discourage courteously
those who are not.*

62. On the Priests of the Monastery

[1]If any abbot wishes to have a priest or deacon ordained, he should choose from his community someone worthy of exercising the priesthood. [2]The person ordained, however, must beware of affectation or pride, [3]and not presume to do anything except what he is commanded by the abbot: he must realize that he will have to subject himself all the more to the regular discipline. [4]Nor, simply because he is a priest, may he forget the obedience and discipline of the Rule, but should make more and more progress towards God.

[5]He should always keep the place which corresponds to the date of his entrance into the monastery, [6]except in his duties at the altar, or unless it is the community's choice and the abbot's desire to give him a higher place on account of his goodness of life. [7]Even so, he should be aware that he will have to keep the rule laid down for deans and priors. [8]If he presumes to act otherwise, he must be judged not a priest but a rebel; [9]and if, after frequent warnings, he does not reform, the bishop also must be brought in as witness. [10]If even then he does not amend and his faults become an open scandal, he should be sent away from the monastery; [11]but only if his obstinacy is such that he refuses to submit or obey the Rule.

This chapter puts clergy in their place and in so doing St Benedict shows an unexpectedly modern approach to the relationship between priest and laity. The priest in his office is – as Christ claimed to be – the servant, one who came not to be served but to serve, the servant of the people of God. All are equally part of Christ, sharing, as Lumen Gentium, *the great document of the Second Vatican Council says, the gift of baptism, the Bible, the Spirit, sharing the life-giving eucharist. All God's faithful people, from pope to the poorest lay person are called to holiness each in his own way (LG: 9, 10, 30, 31, 39). In a real sense we are all priests, through baptism and confirmation, and share in the priesthood of Christ, though not of course a ministerial priesthood.*

St Benedict must have been plagued with the presence of priests who were puffed up with their own importance. Pride he could not tolerate. Plenty of that is around: it comes partly from the competitive society into which we have been born. But self-assertiveness fortunately is counter-productive. Young people seem self-important. It is commonplace knowledge now, that they are often really very unsure of themselves, certainly not proud. They need reassurance, love, to be certain that people care for them, so that they can know they are far from worthless – in fact precious.

But what we all need, in this matter, above all, is to know for sure that God always loves us, that he has given us all the talents we have, that he is happy that we are as we are – not of course our sins, but our limitations – so that we do not have to be too concerned about what the world thinks.

63. On Community Order

April 18
August 18
December 18

[1]In the monastery they should keep the order that corresponds to the date of their entrance, or as determined by the goodness of their lives or the abbot's decision. [2]The abbot must not unsettle the flock entrusted to him nor, by an

arbitrary act of authority, make any unjust arrangement. ³Rather, he must always bear in mind that he will have to account to God for his every decision and action. ⁴The brethren, therefore, should draw near for the kiss of peace or for Communion, or intone psalms or stand in choir, in the order that he has fixed or which they have among themselves. ⁵Furthermore, on no occasion whatever should age settle or predetermine rank, ⁶since Samuel and Daniel were still young when they judged their elders. ⁷Consequently, apart from those already mentioned whom the abbot has for a compelling reason promoted, or on definite grounds demoted, all the rest should keep to the order of their entrance. ⁸So, for example, someone who came to the monastery at the second hour of the day should realize that he is junior to someone who came at the first hour, irrespective of his age or position. ⁹Children, however, are to be kept under discipline in every respect by everyone.

April 19
August 19
December 19

¹⁰The juniors, therefore, should respect their seniors, and the seniors love their juniors. ¹¹When they address one another, no one should be allowed to use just the name alone; ¹²instead, let the seniors call their juniors "brother", and the juniors call their seniors *nonnus*, which means "reverend father." ¹³Yet the abbot, because he is believed to hold the place of Christ, should be called "lord" and "abbot", not out of presumption on his part, but out of reverence and love for Christ. ¹⁴He himself must keep this in

mind and in his conduct show himself worthy of such honour.

[15]Whenever the brethren meet one another, the junior should ask the senior for a blessing. [16]When someone older passes by, the younger person should rise and offer him his seat, and not presume to sit down with him unless his senior bids him. [17]Thus, the words of scripture may be fulfilled, "Outdo one another in showing honour." [18]Small children or adolescents should be kept disciplined and in order both in the oratory and at table. [19]Outside or anywhere else, they should be supervised and kept under control until they come to the age of understanding.

Rom. 12:10

St Benedict is very concerned about mutual respect and this is shown by each monk keeping his rank in the community according to the date of his arrival. But the abbot may change this order if he wishes, to point out in that way the special virtue of some. He is free to do this, though even the abbot is warned by St Benedict not to think he is at liberty to do just what he feels inclined to do in this matter, or set up any order, but himself follow the Rule.

Boys, we find, according to St Benedict, are to be "supervised" in everything and by everyone else too. No uppishness. He had no knowledge of modern psychology. Children have survived both the ancient and the modern ways with them. So perhaps the Rule's approach is no worse than any other.

St Benedict in fact, is sensible on boys, recognizing that they tend to be irresponsible at a certain age. Control them, he says, until such time as they do prove themselves responsible.

The chapter is almost Chinese in its etiquette, the young rising when an elder passes, all calling each other respectfully by special names. Courtesy is the oil in the social machine, the condiment *on the dish, the scent on the clothes. We are, when all is said and done, creatures who communicate by symbols: words, gestures, expression of face – the smile, the raised eyebrows. So Christians or monks and all who are trying specially to see Christ in one another rightly should express their reverence, their respect, in word and act.*

This is one of the places where Communion is mentioned. The others are chapter 38:2 and 10. The scholars are agreed that these refer to Eucharistic Communion, but, strangely to our habits, not to the full Mass. The reason, in part, seems to be that in monasteries, including Monte Cassino, the Eucharist in all its fullness was celebrated only once a week, on Sundays, and also on "Great feasts". The cause was perhaps the dearth of priests in monasteries. This tradition lived on even after monks were normally priests as well, but changed in the later Middle Ages.

However, in our day, when priests are getting rare, Communion may become a regular rite on its own, as it has for the sick. Busy city dwellers, commuters too, may find a Communion Service helpful where the full Mass is not available. Or simply, they could "slip in" for Communion. This seems to have been the original weekday custom in St Benedict's monastery. It is not an ideal arrangement, but in extreme cases possible, with some tradition behind it.

64. On the Appointment of the Abbot

April 20
August 20
December 20

[1]In appointing an abbot, it should always be the practice to place in office someone chosen unanimously by the whole community acting in the fear of God, or even by part of the community, no matter how small, with sounder judgment. [2]The person to be appointed should be chosen for the goodness of his life and the

wisdom of his teaching, even if he ranks last in the community. [3]Yet even if – God forbid – the entire community should agree to choose someone who winks at its evil ways, [4]and these somehow come to the notice of the local bishop, or become obvious to neighbouring abbots and Christians, [5]they must put a stop to this conspiracy of the wicked and set a worthy steward over God's house. [6]They may be sure that they will be richly rewarded if they act from disinterested motives and out of zeal for God; just as, on the contrary, they will be guilty of sin if they neglect to do so.

April 21
August 21
December 21

cf Luke 16:2

[7]Once appointed, the abbot should constantly reflect on the kind of obligation he has undertaken and to whom he will have to give an account of his stewardship. [8]Let him realize that his aim must be profit for others, not pride of place for himself. [9]He must be learned in the divine law, therefore, in order to

Matt. 13:52

know from where "to bring forth things both new and old," as well as being chaste, sober and merciful. [10]He must

James 2:13

always "set mercy above judgment", that he may obtain mercy himself. [11]He must hate evil but love the brethren. [12]When he has to punish, he should do so prudently and not too harshly, for fear of breaking the vessel by rubbing too hard to remove the rust. [13]Let him distrust his own frailty and remember

Isa. 42:3

that "the bruised reed is not to be

crushed." [14]In saying that, we do not mean that he should allow evil-doing to flourish, but rather root it out prudently and with love, in the way that seems best in each case, as we have said. [15]And let him take pains to be loved rather than feared.

[16]He must not be moody or anxious or given to extremes, nor obstinate or jealous or too suspicious, for then he will never be at peace. [17]In his orders he must be prudent and considerate; and whether the task he imposes concerns God or the world, he must be discerning and moderate, [18]bearing in mind the discretion of holy Jacob who said, "If I cause my flocks to be overdriven, they will all die in a single day." [19]Accordingly, taking as his model this and other examples of discretion, the mother of virtues, may he so arrange everything that the strong have something still to wish for and the weak nothing from which to shrink.

Gen. 33:13

[20]Above all, he must keep this Rule in every respect, [21]so that when he has served well, he may hear from the Lord what the good servant heard, who gave his fellow servants wheat at the appointed time: [22]"I tell you solemnly," he said, "he sets him over all his possessions."

Matt. 24:47

This is not the place to enlarge upon the problems in the Rule connected with the election of the abbot. It is certain St Benedict wanted the monks to have a share in the choosing by electing or selecting. He was happy for the local abbots or bishop to intervene should the monks propose or elect an unworthy one. Today the monks elect their abbot and the choice needs to be confirmed by the church authorities.

The really interesting parts of this chapter, from a spiritual point of view, are those describing qualities St Benedict says the monks should look for or avoid in the choosing of their abbot. What the procedure of elections was, has considerable interest for political theorists, as it is one of the earliest models in the emergence of democracy after the absolutism of the Empire.

But here we are interested more in the portrait of the Christian leader or guide, or even spouse. Let us simply enumerate the qualities to be hoped for and those to be avoided, as one chooses an abbot.

The first two qualities are clear and set apart, they are "musts".

1. Goodness of life;
2. Wisdom in teaching.

Then comes the image of "a worthy steward" over God's household. Commentators remind us of Joseph over the Pharaoh's house.

Next St Benedict warns the abbot chosen that he is accountable to God. The abbot's goal must be to profit his monks, not his own pre-eminence. Then St Benedict returns to point 2:

The abbot must be learned in divine law, in order to teach it.

3. He must be chaste, sober and merciful. These virtues go together. They control the emotions and are very necessary for one in a place of spiritual leadership and guidance.

4. Next St Benedict grapples with the problem of firmness and weakness: avoid extremes he says, "set mercy above judgment" (James 2:13). The way to do this is to note the sin, yes, but love the sinner, which he puts thus: "Hate evil but love the brethren". Certain temperaments find it very hard to keep the two separate – the evil done, and the person doing it; the latter is always to be loved.

Even more common is the character who cannot disagree with someone on a point of policy without being angry with the other person, as though to have a different point of view from one's own is morally wrong, wicked.

St Benedict makes two comments here. One is, that too great a severity can make things worse: if you rub too hard in order to be rid of the rust, you can break the vessel. The other is to remember how frail we ourselves are.

Aim at being loved rather than feared. Then comes a list of types of people who are disqualified from the post of abbot: the excitable, anxious, extreme, obstinate, jealous, too-suspicious.

5. *Finally their opposite: he should have forethought, consideration in giving orders, discernment, moderateness, providing the strong with something to wish for, the weak with nothing from which to shrink. It is useless talking about right behaviour if one does not so behave oneself. These many gifts of character are among those we should prize in our companions and dare to pray for in ourselves. This can all very easily be transferred to the secular scene.*

65. On the Prior of the Monastery

April 22
August 22
December 22

¹It has quite often happened that serious conflicts have arisen in monasteries through the appointment of a prior. ²Some, indeed, puffed up by the evil spirit of pride and regarding themselves as second abbots, assume tyrannical power and foster discords and dissensions within the community. ³That is especially the case in those places where the prior is appointed by the same bishop and abbots as the abbot himself. ⁴It is easy to see how foolish an arrangement this is, because from the very outset of his appointment as prior he is given grounds for pride, ⁵since his thoughts will suggest to him that he is exempt from his abbot's authority: ⁶"Well, you

were appointed by the same people as the abbot." [7]This is an incitement to envies, quarrels, slanders, rivalries, disagreements and disorders; [8]and while abbot and prior are at loggerheads, their souls are inevitably put at risk by this discord, [9]and those under them court favour with one side or the other and so go to their ruin. [10]The responsibility for this evil and perilous situation rests on the heads of those who first caused such disorder.

April 23
August 23
December 23

[11]For the preservation of peace and love, therefore, we have decided that it would be best for the abbot to have complete control over the running of his monastery. [12]If possible, every aspect of the monastery should be managed through deans under the abbot's direction, as we arranged earlier. [13]With responsibility thus shared among many, no individual will succumb to pride. [14]But if local conditions demand it, or the community reasonably and humbly makes the request, and the abbot judges it advisable, [15]he may, with the advice of God-fearing brethren, choose whom he likes and himself make him his prior. [16]For his part, the prior must carry out in a respectful manner whatever his abbot lays upon him and do nothing contrary to the abbot's wish or arrangement, [17]because the more he is set above the rest, the more meticulous he should be in his observance of the Rule's requirements.

[18]If this prior should be found to have grave faults, or is led astray by conceit

into arrogance, or is acknowledged to be contemptuous of the holy Rule, he is to be warned verbally up to four times. [19]If he does not amend, he is to be punished in accordance with the discipline of the Rule. [20]If he still does not amend, he is to be deposed from the office of prior and someone worthy put in his place. [21]If after that he is still not a peaceful and obedient member of the community, he must even be banished from the monastery. [22]Yet the abbot should bear in mind that he will have to give God an account of all his judgments, lest perhaps a flame of envy or jealousy destroy his soul.

St Benedict must have had an unhappy experience with priors. He finds they are in danger of being puffed up by their office, particularly if they obtain it not from the abbot but from another source: the local bishop or neighbouring abbots. They become rivals to the abbot, creating rivalry and factions. The Rule lays down that the prior should be appointed by the abbot. Suppose even then that the prior behaves independently, he should be warned as many as four times and then, if he does not amend, let him be deposed.

Life is more complicated in the world, where we may find ourselves saddled with a boss we cannot shake off, or a subordinate who has to be tolerated. Patience is a great virtue; and indeed part of the problem may be ourselves.

66. On the Porters of the Monastery

April 24
August 24
December 24

[1]At the gate of the monastery should be stationed somebody old and wise, who knows how to give and take a message, and whose age will stop him wandering about. [2]This porter will need to have a room near the gate, so that visitors may always find someone there to answer them. [3]As soon as anyone knocks, or a poor person calls out, he should reply,"Thanks be to God," or, "Give me your blessing." [4]Then, with all the graciousness of the fear of God, he should respond promptly, in a warm-hearted way. [5]If he needs help, the porter should be given one of the younger brethren.

[6]The monastery should, if possible, be so constructed that everything necessary – water, mill, garden, the various crafts – may be located within the enclosure. [7]Then there should be no need for the monks to wander outside, since that is not at all good for their souls.

[8]We wish this Rule to be read frequently in the community, so that none of the brethren may plead the excuse of ignorance.

This chapter has many a human touch. A monastery needs a "link with the world" but not one who could lose his vocation in the process. It also needs a friendly type who will receive the visitor with kindness, not gruffly and so alienate him.

He needs to be sensible, one who can take a message, and give a reply. If he were young he might roam about, so he had better be old and stay at the door of the monastery ready to welcome all with either "Thanks be to God" or "Give me your blessing"; all this gently, in the fear of the Lord, and promptly. This is a lovely picture of the spirit in which to welcome guests at the door of one's house, even if today the language may be more prosaic. It shows the warmth of love.

Once again St Benedict is on the look-out in case his monk is over-burdened, in this case, being overwhelmed with guests. Let him have help from the young.

This chapter, as it reaches its end, reads like the first "finale" of the Rule. It reminds us of the end of chapter 20 in St John's Gospel which must have been an early end of that Gospel too. It describes how the monastery should have all it needs within its confines: water, a mill and garden, to avoid monks having to wander outside, which would be bad for their souls. Then comes, "We wish this Rule to be read frequently in the community, so that none of the brethren may plead the excuse of ignorance". Lay people too, can follow the Rule, in so far as it is suitable; they also should read it frequently. In most monasteries a passage of the Holy Rule is read daily, thus getting through it three times a year, on the dates indicated in the left-hand margins in this book.

67. On Brethren Sent on a Journey

April 25
August 25
December 25

¹Brethren who are to be sent on a journey should ask the abbot and all the brethren to pray for them; ²and there should always be a commemoration of all absent brethren at the last prayer of the Work of God.

³When brethren return from a journey, on the same day as they return, they should lie prostrate on the floor of the oratory at the end of each of the customary hours of the Work of God ⁴and ask everyone's prayers for their failings, in case they may have been caught unawares on the road, through

seeing something evil or hearing some idle talk. [5]Furthermore, no one should presume to tell anyone else what he saw or heard outside the monastery, because that does a great deal of harm. [6]Should anyone presume to do so, he is to be subjected to the punishment of the Rule. [7]So also should anyone who presumes to leave the enclosure of the monastery, or go anywhere, or do anything, however unimportant, without the abbot's authorization.

The brethren clearly, as we see from this chapter and others, did go on journeys from their monastery, but only on the order of the abbot. St Benedict is particularly anxious about the spiritual safety of these monks. Both before setting off and after return they must ask the prayers of the abbot and the whole community. He is afraid they may meet with some temptation of sight or hearing that would be a grave risk to their vocation.

If St Benedict is so concerned for the monks just occasionally putting their foot outside into the "wicked world", what must he be thinking of his oblates permanently there? We know that one of the reasons for his flight to the solitude of Subiaco was to escape the great evils of the decaying city of Rome. But the vast majority of people have to remain and face these dangers. God so wills it. Nevertheless we should continually pray not to be contaminated. Both Jesus himself and St Paul tell us to pray continuously. This is what is meant; repeatedly to turn to God when faced with the wanton or cynical attitude of those who have forgotten their Christian roots or sadly never had them. It surely is extremely easy to be contaminated by worldliness, wrong standards, false scales of values.

68. If a Brother Be Commanded to Do the Impossible

April 26
August 26
December 26

[1]If a brother should happen to have something onerous or impossible laid on him, he should accept with perfect gentleness and obedience the command of the one in authority. [2]But if he sees that the weight of the burden altogether exceeds his strength, he must patiently explain to his superior, at an appropriate time, why he is unequal to it, [3]and do so without any pride, obstinacy or argumentativeness. [4]If even after he has put his case, his superior's determination and command remain unaltered, the junior must realize that this is best for him, [5]and trusting in God's help, out of love obey.

This chapter reads like second, and very wise, second thoughts on his fourth degree of humility. What should a monk do when told to do the impossible? The answer is first that with gentleness and acceptance, he should obey. But on reconsideration, if he still knows in his heart that the thing asked of him is a burden which "altogether exceeds his strength"; then what should he do? He should choose the appropriate time, by which St Benedict probably meant, not coming to him before the equivalent of breakfast, or just before he himself was about to set off on a journey, these would be typically inappropriate times. The monk should choose therefore, an occasion when the matter could be discussed at ease, and should "explain to his superior . . . why he is unequal" to the task "without any pride, obstinacy or argumentativeness".

Suppose the superior still holds to his course, what then? The monk must "realize that this is best for him, and trusting in

God's help, out of love obey''. This is the moment of heroic virtue.

A modern monk might say that this is an over-simplified picture and sometimes he would be right. In our time there is the court of appeal. But this only puts off the evil day. The courts of appeal may agree with the abbot. What then? Unless it is a matter of conscience, of sin, one would have to agree with what is written in the Rule.

Does this quandary apply to Christians in the lay state? It certainly does, in so many of the moral problems of our time. The Church makes a decision: on divorce, on birth control, on abortion, on euthanasia, on in vitro experiments. The attitude of mind of Catholics who believe in authority, should be, in gentleness of spirit, to try to understand, and agree; at the same time they should take prudent advice. Moral theologians have written learnedly on many of these moral problems, providing a serious, balanced approach to these very complex as well as extremely important matters. Obviously they are not infallible, but as theologians their judgment carries weight.

Sometimes the decision can be interpreted more benignly than other none too subtle minds will allow. Still, the first response, the underlying desire, should be to listen to the guidance of the Church, itself guided by the Holy Spirit.

We also have to bear in mind the weight of the decision. Not every pronouncement of a bishop or the Holy See is infallible – it is legitimate to remind ourselves of some cases which certainly were not, such as the case of Galileo – nor of course are our own opinions, for that matter, ever infallible. The point remains that we should be extremely cautious about disagreeing with a non-infallible pronouncement (see Lumen Gentium 25).

69. That No One in the Monastery Should Presume to Defend Another

April 27
August 27
December 27

[1]Particular care must be taken that no monk should presume, on any pretext, to defend another in the monastery or take him under his wing, as it were, [2]even though connected by the closest of blood-ties. [3]In no way whatever should monks presume to do this, because it can be a most serious source of provocation and trouble. [4]If anyone should break this rule, he must be punished very severely.

This chapter emphasizes unity among the brethren. To defend a brother against authority is to help create division, and it could destroy the very life of the community. A Benedictine monastery, once the abbot is elected, is an autocracy. But this autocracy is confined within the just bounds of the Rule. There are courts of appeal.

70. That No One Should Presume to Strike Others at Random

April 28
August 28
December 28

[1]In the monastery every occasion of presumption must be avoided, [2]and so we decree that no one should be allowed to excommunicate or strike any of his brethren, unless authority to do so has been given him by the abbot. [3]"Those who sin are to be rebuked in the presence of all, that the rest may fear." [4]Children up to the age of fifteen, however, should be carefully controlled and supervised by everyone, [5]yet this too with real moderation and good sense. [6]Should anyone

1 Tim. 5:20

presume to wield authority over those who are older without the abbot's instructions, or treat the children with indiscriminate severity, he is to be subjected to the discipline of the Rule, *Tob. 4:16* [7]since it is written, "Do not do to another what you do not want done to yourself."

This chapter is a further comment on the government of the monastery. Only those whose duty it is to correct should do so. St Benedict thinks everyone should share in the control and supervision of boys up to the age of fifteen. As always the Rule requires a dispassionate approach and discretion. Rules should be seen to be sensible. Boys should be ruled with all moderation and reasonableness.

71. That They Should Be Obedient to One Another

April 29
August 29
December29

[1]The blessing of obedience ought to be shown by all, not only towards the abbot, but also towards one another in obedience as brethren; [2]for they know that by this way of obedience they will go to God. [3]Consequently, although the orders of the abbot or of superiors appointed by him must come first, and no unofficial commands take their place, [4]for the rest, the juniors should all obey their seniors with complete love and devotion. [5]If anyone is found to dispute this, he should be reproved.

[6]Moreover, if any brother should, for any reason, however slight, be reproved

in any way by his abbot or a senior, [7]or if he senses that one of his seniors is in some way, however small, displeased or angry with him, [8]then straightaway, without any hesitation, he should throw himself on the ground at his feet and lie there, making satisfaction, until the ruffled feelings are soothed by a blessing. [9]Should anyone scorn to do this, he is to be subjected to corporal punishment or, if stubborn, dismissed from the monastery.

We now have reached those last precious chapters of St Benedict's which are quite his own; at least he leaves the Rule of the Master far behind. Here his primary purpose is mutual love, respect and obedience among the brethren. Here, to love is to obey, and to obey is to love. He calls this mutual obedience of the brethren a blessing. It begins with obedience to the abbot but should also be given by all the brethren to one another. Let them obey each other, because, he says, the road of obedience is the road to God.

To obey is to listen intently – looking at the word in its origin – and listening intently issues into action. The root of this Christian, Benedictine obedience is love. We must love our neighbour, one another; truly to love is to do the other person's desires, wishes, will. True obedience is love in act. Therefore apart from the obedience to a superior, which comes first, we should show love to one another, by a loving and caring obedience.

These are thoughts that should apply almost as they stand in any Christian community.

St Benedict is so concerned about this that the very slightest contention, disagreement, dispute, even the very smallest, should be immediately put right by a visible sign of sorrow by the one who has caused it. In a monastery this would be any junior to a senior monk, most of all if caused to the abbot himself. But prostrating in our setting would be over-dramatic. Holy abbots have been known to apologize to one of their own monks for a loss

*of temper. The sign for St Benedict is to prostrate oneself before
the offended monk and so remain until he grants his blessing. We
have to take the customs of our time into account.*

*Here again, any group of Christians can learn from this. The
longer ill feelings are allowed to linger the deeper the canker of ill
will grows and the more difficult it becomes to root it out.*

*In the Rule we find that if the offending monk does not make
amends at once, he is to be disciplined, and if he does not give
way, St Benedict takes so serious a view of it as to demand
expulsion from the monastery. There is almost an infinity of
ways we can show sorrow for being impatient or offensive: by
bringing the post in, or making a cup of tea, a real smile, a mere
touch, just the little phrase, "I'm sorry". Real love shows the
way.*

*He need not explain at this stage of his Rule what he means by
obedience and love, because every word of it has been impregnated
with his clear grasp of the true meaning of both: readiness to do
the will of the other, a turning away from our own wilfulness;
self-giving, not sentimental, lustful, snatching at the other, but
peaceful, chaste, acceptance of others and eagerness to listen to
their needs, spoken or unspoken: the difference between liking
and loving.*

72. On the Good Zeal Which Monks Ought To Have

April 30
August 30
December 30

Rom. 12:10

[1]Just as there is an evil zeal of bitterness which separates from God and leads to hell, [2]so there is a good zeal which separates from evil and leads to God and everlasting life. [3]This, therefore, is the zeal which monks must cultivate with the most ardent love, [4]that "they may outdo one another in showing honour." [5]They must bear one another's weaknesses, whether of body or character, with

the utmost patience; [6]they must be eager to show obedience to one another. [7]No one should pursue what seems best for himself but what seems best for the other instead. [8]They must overflow with chaste and brotherly love; [9]God they must love and fear; [10]their abbot they must love with genuine and humble affection. [11]May they put nothing whatever before Christ; [12]and may he bring us all together to everlasting life.

The language of this chapter is quaint to modern ears: "good zeal", "eager to show obedience" may appear a curious way of describing mutual love, but analyze the thought and it is more realistic than much modern jargon.

Zeal is anything but a passive attitude to others. We might talk of out-goingness; it expresses the eagerness of the heart to help or share with others, so as to bind the community together in love.

The Greek word Zelos has light and darkness in its meanings, which includes, besides eagerness for good, jealousy, rivalry, passion; so St Benedict speaks of good zeal, as here and chapter 64:6, and evil zeal as in chapters 4:67; 55:21; 65:7,22. Thus human relationships can turn sour, which can happen from lack of patience. As St Benedict says, we must support with the utmost patience one another's weaknesses. We recognize that need in each other's physical disabilities, but not so readily the quirks of character or behaviour.

Here again, he equates obedience with love; the brethren are to "be eager to show obedience". He explains here more precisely what he understands by obedience by saying that we must set out to do not what we may judge suits ourselves better, but instead what we judge will be of more use to the brethren.

All this scarcely needs "translating" into a lay context: just as monks must love with a pure love, so should people in the world recognize the distinction in ways of loving. He sums it all up in the final sentence: "May they put nothing whatever before Christ; and may he bring us all together to everlasting life."

73. *That Not Every Principle of Holiness Has Been Laid Down in This Rule*

May 1
August 31
December 31

[1]We have written this Rule in order that, by observing it in monasteries, we may show that we have attained some measure of virtue and the rudiments of monastic life. [2]But for anyone aiming at the perfection of monastic life, there are the teachings of the holy Fathers, following which will lead one to the heights of perfection. [3]Indeed, what page or what passage of the divinely inspired books of the Old and New Testaments is not an infallible guide for human life? [4]Or what book of the holy Catholic Fathers does not insistently urge us towards our Creator by a straight course? [5]Then, as regards the "Conferences" of the Fathers, their "Institutes" and "Lives", and the Rule of our holy father Basil too, [6]what are they for observant and obedient monks but tools for virtue? [7]But as for us, lazy, unobservant and negligent, we blush for shame!

[8]So, whoever you may be, hastening on your way to your heavenly homeland, keep with Christ's help this little Rule for beginners, [9]and then at last, under God's protection, you will attain the more exalted heights of wisdom and virtue described above. Amen.

End of the Rule

This chapter has the only personal comment in the Rule. St Benedict tells us why he wrote it. But the heading itself is a heart's cry, a kind of agonized outburst explaining how inadequate he knows his little Rule is, compared with the Bible itself and the great works of the Fathers. Its contorted style itself expresses this crushing sense of inadequacy.

The heading literally reads: "of how the observance of all justice is not laid down in this Rule", by which he means that in his Rule he has not set out every principle of holiness.

St Benedict is very modest about the value of his own Rule; he hopes it will lead those monks who follow it to "some measure of virtue", but he proposes the teachings of the Fathers for those who are aiming at "the perfection of monastic life". The truest guides are the books of the Old and New Testaments. He then refers to the Conferences – these are generally thought to be those gathered by Cassian during his sojourn among the Fathers of the Egyptian desert; likewise his lives of the Fathers, possibly also others, for instance the life of St Anthony by St Athanasius, and of St Paul the Hermit by St Jerome.

St Benedict ends with a blush for shame that he himself and his followers are so unobservant, so lazy, so negligent compared with the giants of old. He implores those who follow his little Rule for beginners to be faithful to it. But yet we must hasten – a favourite word of his – towards our "heavenly homeland". If we have truly kept his little Rule, then we may move on to "the more exalted heights", and with God's help, arrive there.

Appendix 1: The *Dialogues* of St Gregory

St Benedict's Life

What do we know of St Benedict's life?

He never mentions himself in his Rule. No mention is made of him by his contemporary writers during his supposed lifetime. The first mention of him comes in the volume called *The Dialogues,** in four Books by Pope St Gregory the Great, written in 593–594 in Rome about fifty years after Benedict is said to have died (born c. 480, died 547 A.D.).

The dialogues are delightful, a kind of late Roman parallel to the legends about Francis of Assisi, but written seven hundred years earlier, homely incidents in idyllic settings with many lively tales and a miracle attached.

Benedict according to the Dialogues of St Gregory, was born about 480 A.D. not far from Rome in the province of Nursia, tucked away in the Sabine hills east of the capital.

His family must have been of some standing to have sent him complete with his nurse to the university for study.

Rome was at this point of its history in a parlous state, having been conquered and reconquered several times by northern barbarians and imperial troops from the East. It was not only worn out, it was demoralized; and this was what made Benedict first uneasy and then unwilling to remain. He escaped from its tainted air, not however without the nurse, to a village, Enfide.

---

*St Gregory in his *Dialogues* claims he acquired much of his information from abbots of Monte Cassino after St Benedict's death, from an abbot of the Lateran Monastery in Rome and from the then abbot, when he was writing, of Subiaco.

Benedict's aim seems to have been *solitude* but he did not succeed straight away. First he joined a group of pious Christians just outside Rome at Enfide "leaving the world, becoming knowingly unknown and wisely unlearned". Determined not to be turned into a celebrity as a local wonder-worker, Benedict moved on into the wild country round Subiaco. On the way he met a monk, Romanus, who helped him to find the cave where he lived in solitude for three years.

Romanus promised to help him with bread let down in a basket on a rope from above. No doubt he also lent him books to read. Benedict had temptations of the flesh, and so rolled in brambles and nettles, and overcame these temptations.

Soon some neighbouring monks asked him to be their abbot. Benedict, afraid that he would not succeed, at first refused, but finally gave way. He could not control them, and they in desperation attempted to poison him. At that point Benedict withdrew, returning to Subiaco where, according to St Gregory, he founded twelve small monasteries, as a great number of aspirants by this time had joined him. The parish priest, however, disturbed by this influx, turned against Benedict, who, experiencing this opposition, for peace's sake now withdrew further south to Monte Cassino, which became the great Benedictine monastery. There he wrote his *Rule for Monks* in about 525 A.D. It is this Rule we are commenting upon.

Benedict seems to have passed through the three great stages of monasticism: firstly the hermit or eremitical stage, in the cave overlooking Subiaco, as St Anthony had done in the Egyptian deserts; then the Pachomian stage of several monasteries under his supervision; then the final stage – his own invention of a quasi-family life, a community, under one abbot, himself.

Monte Cassino, half way between Rome and Naples in southern Italy, soon became famous, as according to the Dialogues of St Gregory it was visited by King Totila, a great barbarian ruler, and by Roman senators bringing their boys to school. It was also a centre of evangelizing, as Benedict, though not a priest, would preach to the local pagans.

Very soon before Benedict died, he experienced a vision in the night of brilliant light, as it were from the sun, and in that light the whole world was contained. Gregory in the *Dialogues* explains that when one sees the "light" of God, the whole of creation seems minute in comparison. Compare Julian of Norwich's vision nearly a thousand years later.

Benedict's sister Scholastica used to visit him once a year. Shortly after one of these visits, she died and was buried in the tomb prepared for him. He died, probably in 547, soon after her death. They were buried in the same tomb. That is still there.

St Gregory in *The Dialogues* (Bk 4, ch. 36) sums up his life as follows:"If any one wishes to grasp his character and life better, he will find in the layout of the Rule a complete statement of the abbot's way of life, for the holy man cannot have taught otherwise than as he lived"

Appendix 2: Some Explanations

A. *The Liturgy*

This is the public worship of God by the Church.

The Mass is the central element of the liturgy.

Divine Office, *Opus Dei*, "Prayer of the Church" –
different names for the same thing – is all part of *The
Liturgy*.

Monastic Divine Office, or *Opus Dei*, or work of God,
differs in detail from the "Prayer of the Church". The
former derived from Monastic sources and the "Prayer of
the Church" from cathedral ways of performing it, notably
those of Milan, Rome, Toledo, Lyons, etc., in the West
and Antioch, Alexandria, Constantinople in the Eastern
Church of ancient times. In the West the usage of Rome is
almost universal.

St Benedict quite clearly was organizing a round of
hymns, psalms and readings different in order and in
quantity from the Roman rite, and with an eye on ancient
monastic traditions. The hymns he found in the liturgy of
Milan – known as the Ambrosian rite.

The prayer in one form or another has been going on
since the very beginnings of the Church to this present
moment, when somewhere in the world, at this very
hour, the Eucharistic Prayer, the Mass, is being celebrated
and also the prayers that surround the Eucharist. They
stretch on through the night and the day, on and on in
beautiful harmony of heart and song.

The earliest followers of Christ and his apostles, being
Jewish by race, like him, at first went to the weekly
synagogue meetings, which included psalms and scripture readings. Ever since, this seems to have been the
pattern, though the Christians prayed together daily, in
the family and beyond, both night and day. Our object

here is not to prove it, but to accept the facts established by scholars.

The hermits and monks in groups in the deserts of Egypt, Palestine and elsewhere gradually organized this prayer. We find the culmination of this process of development of the Church's Prayer in the daily prayer as read and sung in the great basilicas of Rome and elsewhere.

The usual pattern seems to have been to place the most important "hours", Morning Prayer and Evening Prayer – they had different names – before sunrise and sunset respectively. But to these the monks in their communities added, spread out through the day and night, Prime, Terce, Sext and None in the day time, Matins or Vigils in the early morning before dawn and Compline in the early night.

B. *The Psalms (Chapters 9–17)*

These are prayers God gave us, coming from the Bible.

They gained their pre-eminence from being ready-made prayer for community use in the Christian Church; partly because they had already been used by the Jewish Christians in their synagogues as the Jews themselves used them. The Christians saw in many of them hints of prophecies about Christ himself: son of David, the king, the mysterious Priest according to the Order of Melchizedek, the suffering servant, and above all the description the psalms seemingly contain of Christ's very passion. And had not Jesus himself used Psalm 21 on the cross as he was dying: "My God, my God, why have you forsaken me?"

Besides, these great poetical prayers, these hymns and spiritual canticles are not all in one key, one mood, one theme. They remind one of a splendid organ upon whose pipes the organist can draw out mighty sounds or delicate plaintive melodies, now a pastoral song, "The Lord is my

Shepherd" (Ps. 22); now majestic tones of praise and love and gratitude; often pleading sounds, as with the beggar at the gate; not uncommonly the clear note of judgment on the rich, consolation for the poor. Each psalm has its own theme: that of the wonder of creation, or of God's presence everywhere, that God loves us all, that he is our Rock, our Shield, our Hope. These are shown in a great variety of ways, especially in the story of God's saving acts in the history of the chosen people. (The Jews were "chosen" in the sense of being a people picked out to carry the promise of salvation for the world, not because they were good. At most times, they represented us all in their sinfulness.)

Some of the Old Testament describes not what we ought to do, but plainly what they did in their day, bad as well as good. So too in the Book of Psalms we find cursing psalms. These rightly shake us: sometimes we may feel a bit like that, but we restrain such thoughts. We are not meant to imitate. With the coming of Christ our Lord we try "to love our enemies". The Psalms became a striking meditation on the true "love and compassion" of God.

The "Prayer of the Church" has omitted some of these, but monks still keep them. Even today, the world around us is ready to live by "an eye for an eye, a tooth for a tooth": retaliation, aggression. Defence of what is just, yes, but unprovoked war, no.

The *Opus Dei* or work of God, the Divine Office for us: God's mercy, our need, our love also, and we say it with Christ, for "where two or three are gathered together in my name, there am I in the midst of them". Christ is our Priest; as Priest he officiates at our communal prayer and especially at Mass. These two are one. He is our leader at prayer, our Priest and Victim in the Eucharist, as the outward sign (sacrament) of his redeeming act.

C: *Monastic Obedience*

Monastic Obedience can only be understood in a Christian sense as love: love of Christ, love of God, love of all for God's sake, as part of his family. This was the last message of Jesus. As St John wrote in his Gospel, "If you love me, you will keep my commandments" (John 14:15).

But again in St John's first letter it is God who loves us first:

"This is the love I mean:
not our love for God,
but God's love for us when he sent his Son
to be the sacrifice that takes our sins away" (1 John 4:10).

The very word obedience has a treasure hidden in its history. If you "unpack" it, *ob audire*, to listen intently, is the language of love. When you really love, you listen intently to know what the one you love wants to happen, and it is done in a flash. So with love for God. You wait upon his word. St Benedict's attitude to loving obedience is precisely that. True Christian obedience to God is done with the speed of love. And he quotes scriptures showing that to obey the Rule or the abbot is to obey God: "He who hears you, hears me".

To obey the one you love is not always easy – we all have our views and plans, and they may collide with those of people we love, with God's plans too. It is the test of love whose views we make prevail.

How do we know what God wants of us? By our consciences, by the Church's teaching, by its understanding of scripture, by the example of the saints, especially St Benedict and his Rule, guaranteed as a sure way of following Christ.

D: *Stability*

Stability became one of the three vows taken by Benedictine monks, all over the world. Before St Benedict's time monks had begun roaming from one monastery to another as the whim moved them, owing no allegiance or obedience to any particular abbey or abbot. This vow is intimately linked with obedience. In the earlier centuries, if you did not get on with your abbot, you walked out and sought one who fitted in with *your* ideas. The two types of monks of this kind were the *sarabaites* or those who got together in twos or threes under no abbot or rule except the rule of their own desire. The most abhorrent kind of monks, so says St Benedict, were those who drifted from place to place, utterly *unstable*. He prefers, unlike "The Master" to say no more. These were the *gyrovagues*.

But an abbot now may well send a monk, for a time, to A, B or C for study, or to give retreats or conferences in the Third World, or away for health reasons. These monks remain stable in the sense of being still under the control of their abbot. And yet St Benedict himself preferred his monks not to leave the precincts of their monastery. Yet again he makes careful arrangements for those who have to go on long journeys.

Stability was a most fundamental need in St Benedict's day; he lived in a world already in collapse, in decay. How could it be restored? So, Benedict restored order, stability in the little world gathered round him. Chapter 58 shows how he set about it with the young who came to find peace. First, would they stay knocking at the gate? How long would they survive in the guest house? Then a wise monk, patient and observant, the novice master, would be put over them. Were they really searching for God, not just for their own ease? Could they stand the ups and downs, the trials? This went on for a year – it still does now. Then they would promise by vow to stay for life. Today a much longer time of trial is the rule.

Our world, a much bigger world, is as unstable as the Roman Empire: Do we truly seek God? How persistently? First and foremost, firmly?

E. Conversatio Morum

Conversatio Morum: how to translate it literally? The Latin words have been under discussion to our own day. What does "*Conversatio*" mean in the context of the Rule? And what are these "manners" he is writing about?

A general agreement has now been reached. The young monk, after a period of trial, vows by his vow to abandon worldly ways, i.e. to change from worldly ways, be converted from them, to the way of the monk, which all recognized in those days as "being withdrawn", into a celibate way of life, and one of poverty and obedience, with, in the case of the Rule of St Benedict, permanent adherence to a particular abbot and place under the Rule. Poverty and chastity are included under "conversion of manners". But while poverty is much discussed in various chapters, chastity is almost taken for granted, except in chapters 4:64, 33:4, 58:25 and 64:9.

In a general way the vow of conversion of manners means changing one's way of life into that of *the monastic way*.

F. *Oblates*

It is not necessary for anyone to be an Oblate, if he or she wants to be helped by following the spirit of St Benedict. Nevertheless it is useful to know what Oblates are, as they help to round off the picture.

In primitive times, that is when the Rule was in the writing (c. 525 AD), children would be brought by their parents to the monastery to be cared for by the monks, and it was presumed they would probably become monks later on. These were the first Oblates. The word means "someone offered" – this would be during the offering of the Eucharist.

That custom has ceased, but the Benedictine tradition of caring for boys has survived in a different form. Many boys are brought up as good Catholic Christians in a great number of Benedictine schools, from Chile and the United States to Hungary and England. The name "Oblate", however, has been transferred to grown-up men and women living the lay life in the world, married or single, who want to share in the spirit of St Benedict and to be linked with a particular monastery of their choice, especially by praying at least part of the Divine Office or Prayer of the Church, and who make a commitment of greater or lesser duration to do so.

Many people in many parts of the world today take St Benedict as their patron, without being Oblates, but hoping to share in different ways in his benign spirit.

G. *Community*

After the first seven chapters, which with the Prologue set the general principles of the monastic life, and which in large measure are taken from a previous Rule, the "Rule of the Master", St Benedict's Rule concentrates on making it possible for the brethren to live together in harmony, in right order. So it deals with the brothers and their abbot, the prayer life, the duties of the various officers from bursar or cellarer to door keeper, from master to guest-master, from infirmarian to children; all these chapters are geared to making the life together so peaceful and ordered that where the goal of all is to love both God and the brethren, as little friction as possible is found. See the chapters on summoning the brethren to counsel (7), on property (33), on obeying one another (70), on Christ himself being "in" all its members (*passim*).

The ultimate goal is that all things may be ordered and at peace – so that all may love God and each other freely, with the minimum of friction.

Some Further Reading

The New Jerusalem Bible, ed. H. J. Wansbrough OSB. London: Darton, Longman & Todd, 1985.

The Desert Fathers
The Lives of the Desert Fathers, trans. by Norman Russell with an Introduction by Benedicta Ward SLG. London; Mowbray, 1981.
The Sayings of the Desert Fathers, trans. by Benedicta Ward SLG. London: Mowbray, 1975.
Derwas Chitty, *The Desert a City*. London: Mowbray, 1966.

The Rule of St Benedict
RB 1980, The Rule of St Benedict. Collegeville: Liturgical Press, 1981. With excellent notes and bibliography.
Basil Hume OSB, *Searching for God*. London: Hodder & Stoughton, 1977.
Esther de Waal, *Seeking God – the Way of St Benedict*. London: Collins, 1984.
Joan Chittister, *Wisdom Distilled from the Daily Living the Rule of St Benedict Today*. San Francisco: Harper & Row, 1990.

Prayer (Various editions available)
Dom John Chapman, *The Spiritual Letters*
Walter Hilton, *The Scale of Perfection*
Julian of Norwich, *Revelations of Divine Love*
The Cloud of Unknowing; The Epistle of Privy Counsel (unknown authors)
Morning and Evening Prayer. Collins: London.

COLUMBA CARY-ELWES was born in London, England, in 1903 and educated in Belgium and at Ampleforth College in Yorkshire. After working in the wine trade in France and in a bank in the City of London, he joined the Benedictine community of Ampleforth Abbey in 1924. He studied modern languages at Oxford University and was ordained priest in 1933. He taught Modern Languages, Political Economy and Religious studies in the College, as well as Theology to the junior monks in the monastery, till 1951, when he was appointed Prior. In 1955 he was made first Prior of the new foundation at St Louis, Missouri, where he was responsible for the building of the new Priory church, which has received international architectural acclaim. He remained at St Louis for twelve years, then returned to the Ampleforth Community. His growing interest in ecumenism and other religions led to his immersing himself in study of the missions in China and Africa, the latter of which he visited off and on from 1969 to 1978, and where he helped to found a small monastery at Ewu in Nigeria.

His published works, besides numerous articles published in periodicals on both sides of the Atlantic, include: *The Beginning of Goodness* (1943, also translated into Polish); *Law, Liberty and Love*, with a Preface by Arnold Toynbee (1950); *Ampleforth and its Origins* (co-editor, 1952), *The Sheepfold and the Shepherd* (1956); *China and the Cross* (1957, also translated into French); *Monastic Renewal* (1967), the product of a series of lectures given at St John's, Collegeville, Minnesota; and *Experiences with God: A Dictionary of Prayer and Spirituality* (1986). His long correspondence with Arnold Toynbee was edited by Christian B. Peper and published as *An Historian's Conscience* in 1987, and he has recently published a volume of *Poems*. He is working on a book on missionary endeavours in Africa, a new work of spirituality and further poems.

CATHERINE WYBOURNE was born in 1954 and educated at Boscombe Convent and Girton College, Cambridge, where she read history. Three years of research, spent mainly in Spain, were followed by three years in banking before she entered the Benedictine community of nuns at Stanbrook Abbey, Worcester, in 1981. She is a member of the editorial board of *Regulae Benedicti Studia*, an international periodical for RB studies, and is currently working on a Latin-English edition of the Rule of St Benedict.

THE CLOUD OF UNKNOWING
Reflections on Selected Texts

Austin Cooper OMI

The writings of the anonymous author of *The Cloud of Unknowing* represent the 'timeless' aspect of the Christian spiritual tradition. Though written in the fourteenth century, they certainly speak to the women and men of today. It is almost as though they were written for our age.

This book contains a series of short reflections on these writings, showing how they relate to the wider Catholic traditions of both East and West, and to the spiritual needs of contemporary Christians. It is hoped this book will be a source of encouragement for all who are engaged in the quest for a deeper prayer life.

The Author

Austin Cooper OMI is a member of the Australian province of the Oblate Fathers and lectures in Church History and Christian Spirituality at Catholic Theological College, Melbourne, Australia. He has a Master of Arts degree from the Catholic University of America and a Doctor of Philosophy degree from Monash University, Melbourne.

by the same Author

JULIAN OF NORWICH
Reflections on Selected Texts

This book offers a series of reflections on the Christian life based on the *Book of Shewings* (or Revelations) of Julian of Norwich, who has her place in literature alongside Chaucer and Langland as well as being one of the great spiritual writers of the fourteenth century. Each chapter begins with a text from Julian, followed by a reflection on the text. The author, who lectures in Church history and in Christian spirituality, reveals the timeless relevance of Julian's message.

TO PRAY AND TO LOVE
Conversations on Prayer with the Desert Fathers

Roberta Bondi

Here is a book that shines like Epiphany amid the welter of works of Christian spirituality.

These conversations on prayer with early monastic teachers, principally the Desert Fathers, illuminate a whole way of praying, living and thinking about life in God's company. The perennial wisdom of the early teaching receives a commentary that is at once earthy, loving and wise.

This exposition of the teaching of the Desert Fathers is extremely well done and very comprehensive. The style is simple and the author succeeds in applying the early teaching to contemporary people and their problems.
— Dom Cyprian Smith, osb, author of *The Way of Paradox*

The Author

Roberta Bondi holds a doctorate in philosophy from Oxford University. She is Professor of Church History at the Candler School of Theology at Emery University in Atlanta, Georgia. She is the author of
To Love as God Loves, published in the United States in 1991.

Books of general Christian interest as well as books on theology, scripture, spirituality and mysticism are published by Burns and Oates Limited.
A free catalogue will be sent on request:
Burns and Oates Dept A,
Wellwood, North Farm Road, Tunbridge Wells,
Kent TN2 3DR, England
Tel (0892) 510850, Fax (0892) 515903

A NEW KIND OF FOOL
Christopher Coelho OFM

Of the making of books on St Francis there is seemingly no end, so why another one? First, because there is no end to interest in St Francis – now more than ever, when he has been proclaimed Patron Saint of Ecology; second, because the author, an Indian Franciscan, brings a quite new freshness of vision to his meditations on the founder of his Order.

The title is from St Francis himself: "The Lord has called me to be a new kind of fool in this world." And St Francis has given the author a "new vision" in his life, one that he sets out here with a unique blend of simplicity, charm and depth – very much in the manner of St Francis himself.

The author sees St Francis as a sure guide to following the one master, Christ – and, "If Christ is our way to God, then people are our way to Christ. Francis took that way. He was not led to people through Christ, as some try to be, who look on other people as an object for practising their love of God on. Francis took people seriously."

This is a heart-warming book that will inspire readers to take other people, and the whole of God's creation, as seriously as St Francis, but with his same sense of joy and celebration.

TO PRAY AND TO LOVE
Conversations on Prayer with the Desert Fathers

Roberta Bondi

Here is a book that shines like Epiphany amid the welter of works of Christian spirituality.

These conversations on prayer with early monastic teachers, principally the Desert Fathers, illuminate a whole way of praying, living and thinking about life in God's company. The perennial wisdom of the early teaching receives a commentary that is at once earthy, loving and wise.

This exposition of the teaching of the Desert Fathers is extremely well done and very comprehensive. The style is simple and the author succeeds in applying the early teaching to contemporary people and their problems.
— Dom Cyprian Smith, OSB, author of *The Way of Paradox*

The Author

Roberta Bondi holds a doctorate in philosophy from Oxford University. She is Professor of Church History at the Candler School of Theology at Emery University in Atlanta, Georgia. She is the author of
To Love as God Loves, published in the United States in 1991.

Books of general Christian interest as well as books on theology, scripture, spirituality and mysticism are published by Burns and Oates Limited.
A free catalogue will be sent on request:
BURNS AND OATES Dept A,
Wellwood, North Farm Road, Tunbridge Wells, Kent TN2 3DR
Tel. (0892) 510850